# HOUSE RABBIT
# HANDBOOK

## How to Live with an Urban Rabbit

# BY MARINELL HARRIMAN

## Drollery Press, Alameda

*To Herman (October 1981—December 1983), our first
house rabbit, whose influence on our lives has
forced us to produce this book.*

Drollery Press, Alameda
in association with David Lewis

Photo credits:
Tania Harriman—pp. 28, 33, 35, 39, 87, 91
Rachael Millan—pp. 46, 47, 49, 85
Wrenn Dabney Reed—p. 66
Amy Shapiro—(photos & prints) pp. 6, 8,
    25, 26, 27, 75, 76
Bob Sharp—(inset) p. 55
Ron Westman—p.53
Photographic prints by Ramell, Inc.

Design: Robert Harriman
Typography: Vera Allen Composition
Printing: Kingsport Press

Library of Congress Cataloging in Publication Data

Harriman, Marinell, 1941–
    House rabbit handbook.

    Includes index.
    1. Rabbits.   2. Rabbits—Anecdotes.   I. Title.
II. Title: Urban rabbit.
SF453.H37   1985   636'.9322   85-25276
ISBN 0-940920-05-0 (pbk.)


DROLLERY PRESS
1615 Encinal Avenue
Alameda, California 94501

# Contents

# Preface

THIS BOOK IS to enlighten you, if you're not already enlightened, on the unique qualities of the rabbit as a house pet. It offers general and specific information on living with house rabbits.

You will find no recipes for rabbit stew, no instructions for pelting and selling rabbit fur and no guidelines of any kind for commercial rabbit raising. This book is for pet owners only.

At the beginning of this writing, based on *my* experience with *my* first house rabbit, I thought I knew about *all* house rabbits. Often I found myself wrong. For instance, I thought originally that I was opposed to a cage of any kind. I've since learned that a cage is not a prison for a house rabbit, who lives in the midst of human activity, often on a living room coffee table. Even if you're away at work all day, this roommate is with you when you brush your teeth at night and when your alarm goes off in the morning. On the other hand, could a rabbit caged outdoors receive as much attention as a by-product of your daily routine? How much time can *you* spend standing at a rabbit hutch in the backyard?

Books on outdoor rabbits will tell you how large to build a hutch and how to take *physical* care of them. Indoors, we are dealing with different animals, and the personalities that develop under human influence are as individual as their human house mates.

## ACKNOWLEDGMENTS

Our deepest appreciation for sharing their house rabbit experiences goes to:

Michael Bass
Randy Chafe
Donna Duguay
Johanna Fateman
Justin Grams
Kevin Holmes
Morgan Holmes
Jim Johnson
Sylvia Johnson
Tamara Leaf
Amy Millan
Lori Peterson
Jack Rosenberger
Victor Rubin
Amy Shapiro
Bob Sharp
Dena Sharp
Robin Sortman
Karen Syme
Betty Tsubamoto
Darcii Tuuri
Erin Urano
Ron Westman
Amy Whitehurst
Beth Woolbright

We thank the Lafayette Pet Shop and Your Basic Bird for helping us find the above house rabbit owners. And our special thanks also go to our health consultants Marliss Geissler, D.V.M., Donald Griffen, D.V.M. and Carol Babington, breeder of show rabbits.

**WHAT IS THAT LITTLE CREATURE SITTING ON YOUR RUG?**
It may elude an answer, but the relaxing time
spent pondering is time well spent.

# PART I: THE PUZZLE OVER RABBIT SENSE

WHO CAN TELL you what a house rabbit is? Biologists can tell you what rabbits are made of and what their organs are like. Stock raisers can tell you what their meat will sell for and what their furs are worth. Show judges can tell you what their physical standards are.

But who can describe the character of a *house* rabbit any better that someone who has shared living space with one?

It was first pointed out to me by Dr. Donald Griffen, a veterinarian, that for the behavior of house-dwelling rabbits, we (the owners) are the experts.

He may be right, I thought. After interviewing other house rabbit owners, I decided that we are indeed experts. Offering our combined experiences and first-hand observations, we can show you what a house rabbit really is.

## EARMARKS OF THE HOUSE RABBIT

Of course you know what rabbits look like, but what do you know of their "minds?" Housed in small heads, their brains have always been considered lacking in mental abilities. Yet, all house rabbit owners can tell you they have witnessed their pets performing beyond their supposed capacities. Perhaps, like other animals in loving human hands,

they are able to fully develop their underrated brains and come up with personalities that no one expects.

Even though personalities and intelligence do vary with individuals, certain characteristics are present in *all* house rabbits.

They are all capable of giving and receiving affection, each in his own way. Some lick, some rub noses and some cuddle. *They enjoy.* They are meticulous groomers. All are inquisitive, and all are capable of mischief. They often like to play—with toys, with other pets or with their human companions. Many play games of their own invention.

You can call it intelligence, instinct, conditioning or whatever, but they can learn to manipulate humans. That beguiling posture of innocence after a misdeed is familiar to any house rabbit owner. They can also learn less intuitive things like how to push with their feet on doors that open outward and to pull with their teeth on doors that open inward. They can learn procedures and how to get what they want. They can learn to use a litter box, to come when they're called, and to sit up and beg for a treat. They can quickly memorize where all the

**TIMID AND DULL-WITTED?**
Trixie replies to such accusations with a bold investigation of the latest in reading material from Amy Shapiro's bookshelf.

snacks are kept, and they're smart enough to be sneaky!

I would find it impossible to label them timid after meeting so many bold rabbits.

Most likely, what has earned them this reputation is their sensitivity and quick response to sharp noises and sudden movements. In other words, they're eas-

Photo by Amy Shapiro

ily startled—as they should be. They're quarry for predators. Yet being alert doesn't always mean willingness to flee. Sometimes they stand their ground or even *attack*. They may be docile but not to the point of being defenseless.

A common peculiarity in rabbits is what my family calls a "down time" during the day. For this long period of lethargy, most house rabbits will seek the solitude of a cage or nap under a bed or some piece of furniture. They will go into an almost trance-like stupor. This is not the best time to show off your rabbit to friends, and it may account for the impression that some people have of rabbits being dull-witted. They are seeing them in down-mode. A house rabbit owner knows what personality hides behind those drowsy eyes and limp ears.

Enthusiasm from the owners of older rabbits shows a pattern in house rabbit development. They all seem to get better with time, and most will go through an exasperating "adolescence" before blossoming into lovable, mature house rabbits. They become easier to manage and can even be housebroken when well past their prime. Often they don't reach their maximum potential for a relationship with humans until after the first year. Unfortunately, many are never given the opportunity to prove it.

## HOUSE RABBITS SPEAK OUT

Animal behavior is subject to a lot of interpretation based on who's doing the research. Pet owners don't have to research their pets' behavior. They live with it and learn its meaning.

House rabbits, of course, bring their native "language" with them when they move into their new country (the house), and the expressions used with each other now have to impart messages to humans. In living with different people, they may develop different "dialects" or even "slang." House rabbit language, therefore, is not limited to the interpretations of scientists studying rabbits in the wild.

More subtle than that of dog or cat, rabbit language can be "read" once the owners are sensitized, especially to body positions. Rabbits use their vocal cords only for emergencies, but they have other ways to communicate. The mood is indicated by the position of ears, tail and feet. The ears may be lazy or alert. They can also be pulled back with tight muscles to look ferocious.

One of the first things to observe is

the grinding of teeth, which I would compare most in spirit to a cat's purr. It accompanies contentment.

Relaxed bunnies often recline with bellies flat and hind legs stretched straight out in back. At the height of contentment, they sometimes roll over and sleep on their sides or backs.

There is no mistaking the affection intended by licking. Another show of affection, often overlooked, is nose rubbing. Many house rabbits like to nuzzle nose-to-nose with their human friends.

Nudging has at least two meanings. One is, Pet or notice me. The other is, Get out of my way.

### FOOT AND TAIL LANGUAGE

Digging has several forms. There's misbehavior digging (like into the carpet), or fun, violent digging into the sandbox, or light digging as a prelude to rolling over.

Thumping is supposed to be a danger signal. It can be confusing to human house mates, who don't see any cause for alarm, and it can be particularly annoying to be warned of "danger" throughout the night.

A thump can also be an announcement. When our house rabbit Daphne was nursing a litter of babies, she would jump into their cage and thump her foot to summon them to dinner.

Herman, our first house rabbit, kept us informed when things were out of place. She thumped whenever the furniture was rearranged.

Rabbits have a lot of expression in their feet. They can be relaxed and crossed or stretched straight out. Toes may spread or curl up in pleasure over being petted. I've seen rabbits playfully kicking from side to side while shaking their heads and flopping their ears. On the other hand, when they simply want to get away, they kick their heels straight up behind them as if to ward off pursuers.

The excitement shown by an erect tail can be caused by anger at an adversary, anticipation of mating (or other affections), and expectation of food.

Another tail expression is a show of defiance. The tail twitches and jerks sideways and, at its worst, accompanies spraying. The less serious and more common version is tail switching, without spraying, simply to "back talk" when being scolded.

Chinning is something we didn't see

**COMMUNICATION AT ITS BEST**
Unmistakable messages pass between the hearts of
those who know this unspoken universal language.

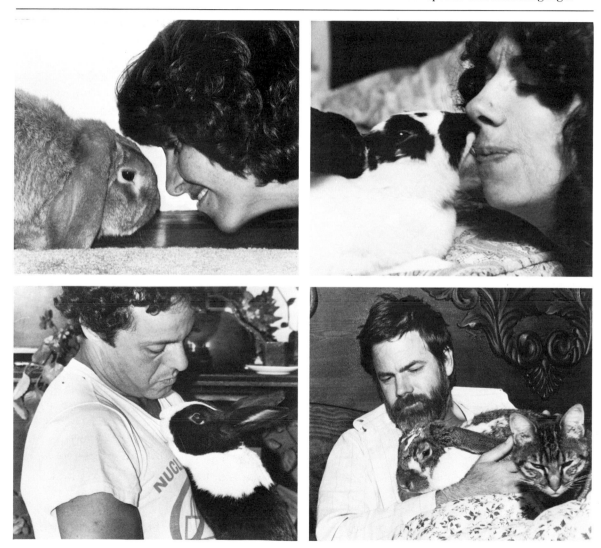

when we had only one rabbit. It is a peculiar way of claiming property. By rubbing their under-chin scent glands on the items they're claiming, they mark them as possessions (undetectable to us). Most of the furniture in our house has been claimed and reclaimed by our rabbit occupants and visitors.

### TEMPER TANTRUMS

Snorting or growling is a sign of anger. It may be just a warning, or it may coincide with an attack. This kind of anger will not occur unless provoked. No animal likes to be teased, and rabbits can be short-tempered when annoyed, but they're not unreasonable about what annoys them.

A less menacing anger is shown by throwing around small objects such as shoes or the food dishes. Most people find this act of rebellion amusing.

Some rabbits "voice" a protest with no more than a few wheezing sniffs, usually when being picked up and carried.

### EROTIC OR OTHERWISE

Since rabbit language has a limited vocabulary, we can expect rabbits to use some of the same "words" with different meanings. This may be perplexing in trying to identify sexual behavior, but interpretation must be based on the individual situation.

Soft "honking" or "oinking" has caused a lot of conjecture. Biologists tell us this is the courting sound of males (based on studies of wild rabbits). Here again, a home environment produces something a little different. I know of many honking females. Most will honk only during "heat" cycles, while others may honk constantly while displaying non-sexual affection (as our first house rabbit did every day of her life). Either way, honking is loving.

Running circles around another animal or a person while honking is considered by scientists to be sexual solicitation. Rabbits use these gestures prior to mating. However, many house rabbits, both male and female, will solicit food and attention in the same manner. After watching many house rabbit courtships in our living room, we do know sexual behavior when we see it and hear it.

The most subtle rabbit expression, often unobservable to anyone but the house rabbit owner, is a smile. That's right. Dog owners have seen this for a long time, so why be surprised that a rabbit can smile?

# PART II: HOUSE RABBIT BIOGRAPHIES

TWENTY-THREE EXAMPLES of rabbits residing with people will be shown in this section. Adding to experience with our own, my husband, Bob, and I visited the homes of other house rabbits. We gratefully accepted facts from their owners, who were among the best people we've ever met. Even in the finest homes, where we'd expect fussiness over the furnishings, there was an easy-going tolerance. No one lost sight of the fun.

All of these rabbits are perfect. They may not all be show quality, and they may not conform to the standards of their breeds, but all conform to the standards of their owners. Photographed in their home environments, these house rabbits are grouped according to their owners' methods of controlling them.

**CONTROL METHOD 1: CAGED IF LEFT UNSUPERVISED**

In terms of controlling a house rabbit, "caged" is not defined by the amount of time spent in the cage, but rather what happens to the rabbit when the owner goes out. Most caged house rabbits are actually uncaged when supervision is available. This could mean anything from ten minutes to several hours a day.

**CONTROL METHOD 2: CONFINED TO ONE OR TWO ROOMS**

This popular method usually requires "bunny-proofing" at least one room. A cage is not always used, but some kind of a door, a baby gate or a pet gate is necessary. Often, additional freedom is allowed under supervision. Some house rabbits are put into cages at night, while others are given a choice.

**CONTROL METHOD 3: UNRESTRICTED**

Success of this method is entirely dependent upon the individual house rabbit's behavior and the tolerance of the owner. More extensive bunny-proofing is usually necessary, but for the right person with the right rabbit, it can be very rewarding.

*Contradictions that exist in various rabbit-owner philosophies are inherent in this open format and therefore intentional.*

# Dinner: *Confidence on the hoof*

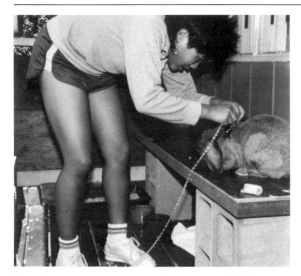

DON'T LET HIS NAME alarm you. This gorgeous eleven-pound golden-red lop is not about to wind up on anybody's dinner table. His owner, Erin Urano, is somewhat of an absurdist, who may enjoy worrying a casual onlooker, but no rabbit has ever enjoyed a more doting "mother."

Erin is articulate, analytical and opinionated. Dinner reflects his owner's confidence. I've never met a more self-confident rabbit. Seeing him walk, harnessed and leashed, to the pet store (to get his toenails clipped), you'd agree there's nothing timid about this guy.

Protesting only a little with squirms and loud sniffs, Dinner can be picked up easily, in spite of his size.

Being quiet and calm, he could easily be ignored by a less sensitive person than Erin. She understands his body language. She knew he was depressed when noisy guests filled their small apartment with cigarette smoke and kept the TV going at full volume.

Not allowing such occasions to arise often, Erin conscientiously provides for Dinner's comfort. Although she lost a phone cord to Dinner's teeth during his youth, he has not been a chronic chewer. She did not bunny-proof her apartment.

Litter box training was a simple matter of providing a box in the same room with the cage and supervising his time out of the cage.

Several months after meeting Dinner, we boarded him for Erin while she was on the East Coast. During that time he fathered a litter of lops for us (page 86) and was given the freedom of our house. His behavior was excellent—a product of his early conditioning.

**FROM SLEEP TO THE STREET**
Dinner emerges from a nap under his bench *opposite* to find himself harnessed and leashed for a stroll to the store *above*.

# Irving: *A healthy addition*

THREE LIVELY POUNDS of chocolate-brown, this charming dwarf with tiny white feet goes by the name of Irving. He lives in a very nice apartment with Karen Syme.

Upon entering Karen's apartment, one would not expect a rabbit to be living there. The oak furniture is free of teeth marks. The velour sofa and the antique braided rug are not in shreds, and the hardwood floors are without moisture spots or stains. Karen even dares to have potted plants on the floor.

Out of his cage, Irving knows which objects are off limits and understands, by the tone of Karen's voice, what is unacceptable behavior. Verbal praise and reprimand are backed up by a few ounces of prevention—in the form of Bitter Apple. A regular spraying makes the furniture, electrical cords and even house plants distasteful to Irving.

Irving doesn't have a separate litter box but returns to his cage for this need. Karen trained him by letting him out frequently for short periods of time.

When Irving was a baby he went to work with Karen, a psychotherapist, and provided some heart-warming experiences for the children Karen worked with. The children had suffered some kind of deprival of a loving situation. Some were at first frightened of the small rabbit, but Karen knew that from Irving they would learn love, trust, care and responsibility.

I commented that adults can now justify owning pets, since we've been told of the benefits to our health.

"Of course," Karen said. "But didn't we know that all along?"

Karen sees a pet as an *addition to* rather than a *substitute for* human relationships. She said that sometimes she may not want to talk to people after working with them all day, and it's better than coming home to her bicycle and more entertaining than the TV set.

Karen's boyfriend, Steve, has a special relationship with Irving—that of the "liberator." The first thing Steve does when he walks in the door is to let Irving out of the cage.

Irving gets plenty of exercise and attention, but he is also able to spend an occasional weekend alone in the cage, allowing Karen to go on short trips. With adequate provisions and toys, Irving is self-sufficient and has proved to be quite capable of fitting into Karen's lifestyle.

**THERAPY FOR A PSYCHOTHERAPIST**
Irving provides Karen with fun and relaxation
after a day's hard work.

# Charlie: *A regular guy*

IT DOESN'T MATTER that at six pounds Charlie is oversized and irregularly marked for a Dutch rabbit. He is personality-perfect.

When I met Charlie he resided at the Lafayette Pet Store under the care of Morgan Holmes. Morgan and his younger brother Kevin are experienced with rabbits. They work every day after school in their father's pet store. Their way of training Charlie was the same as it would be done in a house.

Charlie was kept in a mid-sized cage, and when things weren't too busy, he was turned out to run. Morgan noticed that there was very little cleanup.

Charlie was so good he deserved a lot of treats. He was given carrots and hay for his chewing pleasure and, of course, his favorite snack, unshelled peanuts. Other chewing had to be carefully controlled, where aisles of pet supplies offered many temptations.

For a toy Charlie was given a large, limp towel that he would scoot around with his front feet, then pull and tug on it with his teeth. After that he would

bunch it up and dig into it as though it were a pile of sand.

After endearing himself to all who entered the store, Charlie was offered a permanent home with the right family.

**CHOOSING CHEWS**
Charlie's bag of chomps *opposite* is quickly replaced by Morgan with a towel-toy *right*.

# Peaches & Buns: *Twin Companions*

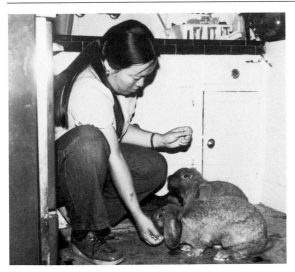

VERY OFTEN a rabbit owner wants a second house rabbit after the first proves to be wonderful. By that time it's difficult to introduce a newcomer, when number-one rabbit doesn't want competition.

Betty Tsubamoto had sense enough to buy two baby rabbits in the first place, even though she said it was an impulse buy. Few of us have that much foresight on an impulse. She wanted her pets to have each other for company while she was away at work all day.

Peaches and Buns are pretty, little gold lops, whose personalities match their looks. When I met them, they were one year old, and I was curious to see if house rabbits with each other for companions would relate as well to people. These two were friendly with each other, with Betty and with me. Since then Betty has told me that they're becoming more affectionate all the time.

Betty raised them with a litter box (a small baking dish) inside their cage. Their routine is to remain in their cage while Betty is at work. She lets them come out whenever she's at home, evenings and on weekends, but limits them to the kitchen unless she can supervise.

The kitchen—with its two rabbits, cage, litter box and supplies—is super clean (like the rest of her apartment). For storage containers she uses plastic pails with snap-on lids, sold in most department stores. One size is perfect for a 25-pound bag of pellets, and a larger one is perfect for wood shavings. Betty has avoided the mess that some of us go through and has proved that it's possible to raise two rabbits in an apartment kitchen and keep it tidy.

**HAPPY WITH HANDOUTS**
Peanuts from Betty's hands are special to Peaches and Buns *above*. On the other hand, Peaches passes over a peanut on the floor *opposite*.

# Mercedes: *A lady of quality*

WHEN BOB AND I entered Tamara Leaf's apartment, a large, friendly French lop came to greet us. My first thought was, What a wonderful animal! Mercedes was the first full-size lop that we had seen, and while she may look like our mini-lop, her movements are much different. She comes when she's called and carries her twelve pounds in a graceful ripple, or rather a wave, from front end to back.

Orignally purchased by Tamara over three years ago, Mercedes is now shared by Robin Sortman, who takes an equal part in her pampering.

When Mercedes is completely relaxed, she rolls over to get her belly rubbed and often licks to show her affection. Her favorite toys are shoes, and her favorite treats are melons and chocolate (not together). Her way of begging for a treat is to run circles around Tamara's or Robin's feet in front of the refrigerator. "Whatever gets us to respond, she'll try," Tamara told us.

Mercedes was trained to newspapers before she graduated to a litter box, which she uses when she is out of the cage. She is supervised and given things to chew during her free time, and the apartment doesn't require bunny-proofing.

Mercedes has a special brush and toenail clippers, which take care of her grooming. Although she's in perfect health now, she caught a cold once during her first year when she was left on the porch just prior to an abrupt weather change. Later she suffered an ear infection, for which Tamara gave her injections prepared by her veterinarian. Tamara has not forgotten how she suffered along with Mercedes through those early illnesses.

Mercedes recovered to a life of being rewarded, indulged in and catered to constantly.

**FASHION FIT FOR A QUEEN**
Mercedes sits regally with her white fluted collar *opposite* and accepts her due respect from Robin Sortman *below* and Tamara Leaf *inset*.

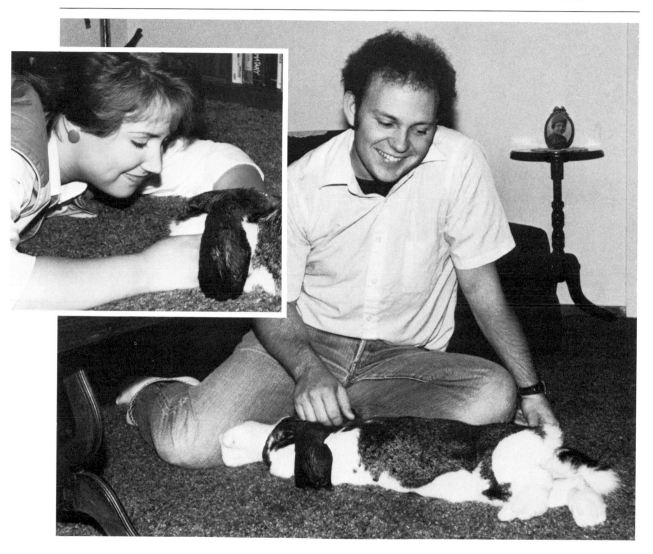

# Trixie & Oscar: *Friends at last*

AN AMENABLE MIX of Netherland dwarf and red satin, Trixie and her lop friend, Oscar, romp through the rooms of the upper floor of Amy Shapiro's house. Although they have evolved into uncaged house pets, they are included here because they started out as caged rabbits with carefully planned living accommodations and were trained by the caged method. Amy had designed and built an indoor rabbit pen, complete with a play house, toys, litter box, resting boards and open areas.

When making the switch to the uncaged method, she gave them plenty of alternatives for their chewing needs. It was Amy who first told me about clear plastic tubing for bunny-proofing electrical cords (described on page 83). I have her to thank for saving our computer and maybe our rabbits' lives.

**ANIMAL WELFARE**

There is nothing haphazard in Amy's dealings with pets. Outside her home she also works toward the well-being of animals. She serves as a volunteer for the San Francisco S.P.C.A., where her talent as a photographer is quite useful in placing pets eligible for adoption.

With sympathies for the plight of the many animals that are destroyed on a regular basis, Amy had originally wanted a cat but decided on a rabbit because her boyfriend, Victor Rubin (page 6), is allergic to cats. He has had no allergy problems with her rabbits, however.

When I first met Amy, Trixie was seven months old, and Oscar had not yet moved in. Trixie licked and nudged me and practically melted into the floor when I petted her. I was surprised to hear that she had once been shy.

Amy was first to make me aware of rabbit adolescence. What can better explain that troublesome period between four and six months? We all agree that we start out with these tiny angels that grow into mid-size devils before they grow into the full-size, easy-going companions that we know and love.

When Amy brought in Oscar, a friendly little lop, Trixie did not accept him. Amy had to keep them in separate cages, or the fur would fly and they'd both wind up with severe scratches. She found she had to make many decisions—when to let them be together, when to let one or the other out for some time around the house, and at what point in a scuffle to separate them. She couldn't

**MASTERPIECES IN ART**
Trixie fits the design motif of the house she lives
in as well the lifestyle of the people she lives with.

Photo by Amy Shapiro

**INTRUSION OF THE ALIEN**
Suspiciously, Trixie eyes young Oscar through his cage *above*. She has come a long way to her present demonstration of acceptance *opposite*.

# "A few weeks later, Trixie returned the favor, and I knew I was home free."

### RABBIT FRIENDSHIP

*Two rabbits are more than twice the fun of one. Every time I see Trixie and Oscar stretched out next to each other, I remember the early weeks, when I kept asking myself, Is it worth it? Will they ever get along?*

*I had no idea what to expect when I brought home 5-week-old Oscar to meet 10-month old Trixie. When she saw him, Trixie took one sniff and then lunged, growling. I scooped up Oscar and put him in his cage. Since then I've spent a lot of time choreographing their movements.*

*A week after Oscar was neutered, I started to see some progress. They still chased and nipped at each other, but they also spent time sitting quietly. One day I saw Oscar lick Trixie's face. A few weeks later, Trixie returned the favor, and I knew I was home free.*

*Now, a year and a half after bringing home my first rabbit, I have two rabbits, who are best friends—to each other and to me—who are never confined to a cage, and who have taught me that patience and a willingness to watch and learn are the best ingredients for getting to know creatures of any species.*

*Amy Shapiro*

find any information on how to introduce rabbits to each other and had to rely on methods of trial-and-error.

As Oscar sexually matured, Amy had another cause for keeping them separated. Not wanting to take any chances, she had Oscar neutered at 3 1/2 months of age and gradually allowed them to run together. They began to sit three feet apart, then two feet, and now they're practically inseparable.

Photos by Amy Shapiro

# Daphne: *Unruly innocence*

A REAL LAP BUNNY, Daphne is an eight-pound agouti and white lop who lives with us. Bob and I are a middle-aged couple enjoying "babies" in the house again. Child substitutes? Of course. But we've already raised two human children, and this seemed a harmless outlet for our continued parenting needs.

For a caged rabbit, Daphne has a lot of freedom. She is uncaged evenings, when we're all home, and frequently during the day, because I have a home office/studio and can keep an eye on her.

When I'm doing work that requires heavy concentration, I put her back in the cage, because watching her is not always that easy. She is meddlesome at times and likes to get into things, and she's not afraid of heights! She often lunges onto the tops of tables, dressers and desks, causing considerable disarray and maintaining a look of blameless innocence all the while. She begs at the dinner table, and if our daughter Tania doesn't slip her a treat, she's likely to jump right onto the table and help herself to the salad.

We also have to watch our coffee cups. If we leave them sitting around the house, she will leave us very little for ourselves.

Daphne is one of the few rabbits we know that actually likes to be picked up and held. She licks our hands lovingly, and we forgive her for all her misdeeds. We take her, in her cage, to visit Bob's mother twice a week. Daphne's behavior doesn't warrant letting her run loose in other people's houses, and she knows not to expect it. After dinner she is passed around to sit on our laps in front of the TV, and this she seems to enjoy.

Her sweet disposition may be due to being "used" during her first few weeks with us. We were grieving over the death

Photo by Tania Harriman

**LEISURE ANGEL OR LIVELY DEVIL?**
Daphne's lounging innocence *below* is discarded for
a salad bowl *opposite*, which our daughter has left
on the table "inadvertently" until last.

of Herman, our first house rabbit, and we turned to Daphne for comfort and held her constantly. She got us through those miserable times and became accustomed to being held in our arms.

In the beginning of our relationship, I was disappointed that Daphne was timid. She had a tough act to follow. I had to learn again (as I had earlier with my children) that the needs of individuals aren't always the same. Daphne needed a lot more reassurance and the security of a cage. I knew nothing about caged rabbits.

**TRUE CONFESSIONS**

We made a lot of mistakes in training Daphne, and I'm willing to confess them all, because it might save other rabbit owners from the same ones. First, we gave her too much freedom too soon. She was frightened and bewildered by her forced freedom, and it delayed her progress.

Since Herman had slept on our bed, we also tried to push Daphne into the same pattern, again too soon. Confused as to what we wanted, she thought of the bed as a giant litter box. In fact she had trouble distinguishing any soft cushions or bedding from litter box material. We had to take drastic measures to break her habit,

and we banished her from our bedroom for a while. She now sleeps caged at night a few feet away from our bed.

Daphne made some progress in toilet training from age five to seven months. She has good bladder control unless she's in heat or has been upset. She is rather nonchalant about her pills and does scatter a few. She has never particularly liked sitting on her litter box for long periods of time, probably because of too harsh discipline during her training. I used to grab her abruptly and yell at her while putting her on the box. She then associated the box with unpleasantness.

All has not been lost, however. She is beginning to like the litter box. I've found that keeping it very clean has made a big difference. Fresh cat litter in the box seems to make her want to get into it. As it begins to get packed down, it loses its appeal.

I stopped scolding her for scattered pills, since it's so easy to sweep them up.

The completely different approach that we had to take with Daphne made us aware that there is more than one right way to raise a house rabbit. She caused us to look at the other rabbits included in this book, and we truly thank her for that.

# Lullabye: *An agreeable responsibility*

AT TWO YEARS OLD, Lullabye weighs about seven pounds and lives in Johanna's upstairs bedroom. My daughter went with me to meet ten-year-old Johanna Fateman and her delightful mini-lop, Lullabye. He was the first neutered rabbit that we had met, and we were very impressed by his pleasing disposition.

Lullabye can be picked up easily and will sit on Johanna's lap as long as she wants him to. We have not seen a rabbit owner, of any age, more capable than Johanna at handling her rabbit. At first I thought her approach was timid, until I saw that her patient manner was actually a show of strength. She has the confidence to be gentle. She manages him by persuasion rather than force, and she gets results.

Lullabye is very affectionate with his young owner. He licks her face and nibbles on her hair. Often he jumps into bed with her, and if he finds her reading a book, he will nudge it aside so that she will pet him. If he needs attention during the night, he wakes her up by jumping onto her back. She said this was startling until she got used to it.

Johanna attributes Lullabye's sweet temper to neutering. She says he's even

**PUTTY IN HER HANDS**
This lovable lump wouldn't dream of biting, kicking or scratching his young owner, who holds him in an unconventional but effective way.

# "She returned home to find him out in the room, but with no spots on the floor."

more affectionate than before. He had been somewhat aggressive and nipped at people's feet and sprayed a little. He now gets along with any of Johanna's guests, including her friend's dog.

He still snorts and growls, but to Johanna's amusement, it's only when he's by himself in the cage. She says he gets into his cage and practices. Maybe he's afraid he will forget how.

For toys she gives him parrot wood that she buys in the pet store. She protects her electrical cords with plastic tubing, but he doesn't bother the toys and books on her bookshelf.

Lullabye spent his early months in his cage, where Johanna noticed that he used one corner for a "bathroom." When he started getting out, he would return to it instead of going on the floor. Johanna learned this by accident one day when she left the cage door open and went to school. She returned home to find him out in the room, but with no spots on the floor. Johanna lines his cage with newspapers, which she changes daily. No litter material is necessary.

Johanna has complete charge of Lullabye. She had to sign a contract with her dad before she was allowed to have a pet. She told us that when she was little she was restricted from her sister's outdoor rabbit, because she squeezed it and pulled its tail.

"But when I was eight, I became responsible," she told us, "and my parents decided to give me another chance."

I'm sure her parents have never regretted giving Johanna another chance. She's responsible, and she cares. Lullabye can tell you that.

**HAPPINESS IS A GOOD SCRATCH**
Johanna scratches the top of Lullabye's head *above* to his obvious satisfaction, but he manages his own chin *opposite*.

Photo by Tania Harriman

# Phoebe: *Affection in disguise*

OUR FEISTY SPOT rabbit lives, completely uncaged, in our kitchen and has access to a small porch at the back. At seven pounds Phoebe seems small to us but full of mischief. She is not allowed in the living room for two reasons. She is an avid chewer, even for a rabbit, and she doesn't get along with Daphne, our lop, who occupies the front of the house.

Phoebe uses a flat tray for a litter box, because she chose a corner for it where a door has to open over it. I have to change it daily, since it can't be piled high with litter. Being adamant on where she wants her box, however, she is equally reliable about using it.

She's rowdy, aggressive and kind of ornery. She charges at people who enter the kitchen and nips at their shoes. She bites, kicks and scratches when provoked and snorts and growls if you cross her.

Why do we keep such a mean rabbit? Take a second look. For all her fierceness, she's aggressively affectionate. She may bite your shoes, but put your face next to hers, and she will smother you

with kisses. Her meaness is just an act of bravado. Her kicks and scratches are gestures in the air. Even her bites aren't real, but rather, bold grabs with precise control. She can take my hand in her razor sharp teeth and move it without leaving the slightest mark.

She can even be gentle if she chooses. While detesting most rabbits, she loves cats and dogs. Happiness for Phoebe is raising a kitten.

She hates to be picked up but will come when she is called and hop onto our laps (provided we don't try to hold her there). Mean or not, she's never a bore.

**HER OWN BAG OF TRICKS**
A lurking, likable villain waits to surprise her next victim *opposite*. It may be a pair of shoes, or a wagging dog-tail, or a whole cat *above*.

Photo by Tania Harriman

# Tiffany: *A reflection of comfort*

IN MOST CASES we've included house rabbits past the age of six months, so that we could be certain that the owners had gotten past the most troublesome times.

I made an exception for Tiffany, since she was Amy Whitehurst's second house rabbit. Amy's first rabbit had already shared the large upstairs bedroom with her, and Amy was well prepared to care for this gentle little white lop.

Tiffany's home is filled with cushions, rugs and comforters—quite plush for a rabbit. She can sit quietly and gaze at the aquarium or join the cat on the window sill. She shares a litter box with the cat and uses her open cage solely for eating and sleeping.

When I first saw the little pink-eyed rabbit with a pink bow around her neck, sitting like an ornament on the thick cobalt-blue carpet, I felt uncomfortable with what I thought to be unrealistic perfection. Then Amy began to show me her problems, and I could relax.

She lifted the bed covering to expose a few teeth marks in the wooden frame and several feet of electrical wiring that she had taped, re-routed or covered up. Behind the door she showed me a tiny edge of carpeting that had been dug up. In box training also, Tiffany had suffered one or two regressions—on an overstuffed chair that was temporarily removed.

Tiffany's errors were becoming fewer, however, and Amy thought of her as a "good" house rabbit.

Amy does not consider paper a suitable chewing material for rabbits, because of potential intestinal blockage. Instead she brings in branches for chewing alternatives. "Beyond that," she said, "you just have to live with a few things." Very well put, I thought, and couldn't we all use that same kind of tolerance with people as well as pets?

**LUXURIOUS LIVING**
Relaxing in her carpeted cage *opposite* or reveling in Amy's attention *below*, Tiffany is accustomed to "the good life."

# Elliot: *Brother to a cat and dog*

WHEN MY DAUGHTER and I photographed Elliot, he weighed about 7 pounds. He was five months old and at the peak of his adolescence. His owner, fifteen-year-old Darcii Tuuri, dealt with him as an indulgent, loving, yet disciplinarian mother. She conditioned him not to chew the cords in her bedroom, which was shared with a tabby kitten, and supervised his activity in the rest of the house.

I noticed that Darcii had placed a light towel on top of Elliot's cage so that he wouldn't catch his toes in the wire as he jumped in and out. This seemed like a good idea. I had once rescued Daphne from this kind of "toe trap."

When I checked back with Darcii after Elliot was fully grown, the family had moved into a new house. Elliot and his younger "brother," the grown-up kitten named Mayo, now share a bedroom in the garage adjoining the house. This gives them plenty of romping space during the winter, and Elliot comes into the main part of the house under supervision.

During warm weather, Darcii and Elliot spend a lot of time in the backyard. They have been joined by an Australian Shepherd puppy named Whiskey, who keeps the yard safe for Elliot.

Additional recreation can be found in a backyard wood pile, where Elliot can get unlimited chewing.

Darcii says Elliot has become more affectionate as he's gotten older. He's a nose nudger, who also likes to have his ears scratched. He tells Darcii to rub his ears by shaking his head and flopping his ears against her. This seems a unique expression in rabbit language that he has developed for Darcii alone.

**COUCH, CUSHION AND CUDDLY COMPANION**
What more could a rabbit ask for? Elliot rumples his favorite cushion *opposite* and is cuddled by Darcii, his favorite person *above*.

Photo by Tania Harriman

# Blue: *A paragon of patience*

AUSTRALIAN BORN, Sylvia Johnson says that the custom where she is from is to call a redhead "Blue." What else then would she name her red rabbit?

Blue is a quietly lovable mini-lop, who shows his fondness for his owners, Sylvia and Jim, with gentle nudging, grunting and by circling their feet. He likes to be with people and knows when it's the right time for attention.

Blue's area of confinement is a large kitchen, a back stairway and a small

## ROOM AT THE TOP

Blue's upward climb every morning
takes him to Sylvia and her attention
*above*. Blue waits patiently for
a frolic with Jim or the gift
of a new toy *opposite*.

# "He senses when dinner is almost over and begins to nudge or sit up in expectation."

guest room at the top of the stairs. That's quite a bit of running room for a seven-pound rabbit. Blue begins his day by climbing the stairs and waiting for Sylvia at the bedroom door. He then follows Sylvia back down the stairs to the kitchen, where together they put on the teakettle.

This is Blue's special time with Sylvia, who spends most of her day at work as a material designer. Her husband Jim, a metallurgy professor, has a special time with Blue during the evening.

Sylvia's fondness for rabbits dates back to her childhood in Australia, where because of rabbit over-population, rabbits were illegal to own. She and her brother and neighborhood friends kept "undercover rabbits" for pets. They had to be constantly alert and keep their rabbits well hidden, or they could lose them in an unexpected police raid.

When Sylvia went away to college, she didn't know that uncaged rabbits could be managed indoors. Blue is the first one to be housebroken and to have the kind of freedom he enjoys. Blue has Jim to thank for this. When Blue was five months old, Sylvia had to be away for ten days, leaving Jim to baby-sit.

The normally quiet bunny became in-tent on rattling his cage at night, and Jim opened the door every time Blue got noisy. When Blue saw that he could go in and out as he pleased, he did not hesitate to return to his "toilet" in the cage.

Sylvia returned home to a housebroken rabbit and a husband who was willing to take the necessary steps to bunny-proof a section of the house. The kitchen phone cord is enclosed in On Wall Wiring.

As for mishaps, Blue has suffered one close call by eating too much paper and causing a blockage in his digestive tract. He had to spend the night in the hospital but is now well recovered. On the advice of her father, a botanist, Sylvia has also put apricot leaves and potato peels on Blue's list of non-edibles.

Blue has settled back into his routine and waits under the table in the evening. He senses when dinner is almost over and begins to nudge or sit up in expectation. It's Jim's time to play with him.

Blue sees a lot of Sylvia and Jim on weekends, since they spend most of their time at home.

When the Johnsons invite friends over for the evening, Blue comes out of the kitchen to co-host and to do his part in providing the entertainment.

# Ninja: *A small wonder*

BECAUSE OF MY OWN experience with large rabbits, I was convinced that dwarfs were fragile and, of course, not rugged enough for kids. Then I met Ninja. Here's a bouncy two-pounder with no intention of being delicate. He pals around with his nine-year-old owner, Justin Grams, as well as the other friends Justin brings home.

Justin is Ninja's main human companion, who shares friends, floor, toys, TV and pretzels with him.

Ninja's home is the kitchen, but he's allowed in the living room when the family is home to provide supervision.

The Grams family did not bunny-proof the living room because Ninja is there only under supervision. Some work was required in the kitchen. Ninja took a fancy to the phone cord. After watching it being spliced, he smugly chomped through it again. Now, instead of a phone cord dragging across the kitchen floor, it runs vertically up the wall, enclosed in a 2-foot-long plumber's pipe. The exposed cord at the top of the pipe is out of Ninja's grazing range.

Justin had help from his mom, Elinor Grams, in box training Ninja. They found that housebreaking was not just a simple

**WHAT'S MORE AMUSING THAN TV?**
Ninja competes with the TV for the attention of Justin and his friend Dana *above*.

matter of setting out a litter box. Perhaps the high sides were discouraging to him at his size. It seemed a hopeless undertaking until they tried a new approach. They put Ninja back into his cage for a few days and allowed the tray underneath to become thoroughly dampened. They removed the tray and then set it in the corner for a daytime litter box, and after finding it marked with his scent, Ninja knew what it was for. Now that Ninja has 100% urine control, no one

**WANT TO GET ROLLED?**
Ninja's hamster friend Earnie is fun with and
without his exercise ball *below, left and right* and
much less dangerous than his paper cup *opposite.*

minds picking up a few scattered pills.

Since Justin was used to hamsters, he
knew he didn't mind keeping up a cage.
He chose a Polish dwarf, so that it would
be compatible with his hamsters, but
since then he has found it to be more of a
companion to him than he had
anticipated.

Justin's mother tells of an amusing little game they play. Justin will say, "Come
on Ninja. Let's play cops and robbers."
Ninja knows that means it's time to play.
As Justin points his "gun" (a finger) at
him, Ninja takes the cue and goes into
his little act. He makes running leaps in

the air and kicks his heels from side to
side. Whether or not Ninja knows he's
the "robber," he loves the romp.

Another game Ninja enjoys is nudging
his hamster friend along in an exercise
ball. Ninja has many toys to choose from,
like shoes, cereal boxes and paper bags.
His favorite, however, is a paper cup that
he likes to carry around. Sometimes Justin puts a few Cheerios inside, which may
cause Ninja to reach in too deep and
wear his cup on his nose.

There seems to be no limit to the fun
that Ninja brings to the Grams household.

# Agarami: *The charismatic comedian*

A WHIMSICAL LITTLE show-off, Agarami has found himself in an unlikely home—unlikely because the Millan family had never owned a pet before.

Amy Millan, our son's companion all the way through college, has spent so much time with us that she was bound to catch rabbit fever. Amy decided a bunny was to be her mother's Christmas present.

Truthfully, I was a bit worried. A rabbit for a *first* pet? But Amy trusted her family's ability to adapt. She chose a mixed breed, part checkered giant, with a persuasive personality and theatrical eyes. She then flew home from Berkeley to Los Angeles with her "surprise."

It turned out to be more than just a surprise. It was a real shock. Amy said it was the last present to be opened. When her mother pulled back the blanket that covered the cage, she let out a scream, thinking it was a rat. When things calmed down, the bunny was passed around, while careful consideration was put into the choosing of a name. Alma, Amy's mother, decided his name would be

Agarami, a coined word from Angelo, Gina, Amy, Rachael, Alma and Mitzi—every member of the family. At first the girls protested that it was too long, but their dad insisted that they keep the name that Alma had chosen.

Amy knew what she was doing when she selected a white rabbit. She describes her mother as being "into cleanliness." Things may get cluttered in their day-to-day living, but everything is spotlessly scrubbed and shiny clean.

When the time came—as it usually does for people unfamiliar with the concept of house rabbits—her dad said,

**A WORLD TO SEE AND CHARM**
Agarami leaps freely out into his "world," the family room *opposite*, and Alma discovers the amusement of a new world on her floor *above*.

Photos by Rachael Millan

# "He jumps over stomachs, chews hair, licks faces, gets under blankets and is great to have around."

"Well, let's put him outside."

"Oh, no!" his wife quickly objected. "He will get all dirty!"

Amy had introduced a house rabbit. We followed the story with anxiety, grimacing when we heard he had chewed up a bit of drape, but rejoicing when we heard he was being forgiven and trained, not thrown out. He's quite an intelligent rabbit and learns quickly.

Agarami's home is a large bunny-proof family room. His teeth get a good workout on fresh tree branches, twigs and logs that are routinely brought in for his chewing satisfaction.

Evening TV hours in the Millan house are 8:00 to 11:00. With the kids in the family room, Agarami is ecstatic. He jumps over stomachs, chews hair, licks faces, gets under blankets and is great to have around.

Although he may have done a little chewing on some curtains or slippers, he has left a large teddy bear intact. He likes to crawl onto the teddy bear and sleep on its legs.

When Agarami was five months old, he came back for a visit, and we were able to observe this zesty little rabbit in action. His flamboyant gestures give him the appearance of a cartoon character or even a miniature person pretending to be a rabbit. He waves his "arms" around and uses his front feet almost like hands.

Agarami can be picked up easily but is too active to sit on anyone's lap for an extended period of time. On the other hand, he is generous with loving licks.

**BENEFICIAL SIDE EFFECTS**

Amy was most concerned over her dad's approval of Agarami as a house pet. Even being a doctor, he wasn't sure at first about the health benefits. Now, he feels it's good therapy for his wife, who has high blood-pressure. Instead of lying on the couch in front of the TV, she is down on the floor petting the rabbit.

Amy's family has always been concerned over Alma's high blood-pressure, and they try to avoid any causes of stress. The strange thing about a pet for therapy is that it works the opposite to what you'd think. The change that Amy has seen in her mother is that she has become more easy-going. Things that would have bothered her (like a little chewed curtain or a few scattered pills) are not so important. These are powerful little pets to alter such firm values as a spotless house.

## HIGH PERFORMANCE
Demands on an entertainer—high sitting *top left* or walking high on all fours *lower left* or sometimes stretching to a two-legged stand *right*.

Photos by Rachael Millan

# Sesame: *An outgrowth of art*

NOT ALL HOUSE RABBITS get to romp in a hose tower, but that's what Sesame does. She lives with Donna Duguay and Ron Westman, both artists, who dwell in what was once the Alameda fire house.

Our first visit to the Westmans was on a cold winter evening, and the only heating came from a wood stove in an upstairs kitchen, or all-purpose room. Bob and I had been shown through Ron's downstairs studios, which were large enough to house several fire trucks as they had in the late 1800's. At the top of an open ladder-type staircase is a landing which serves as a living room, off of which is Donna's studio where as an artist she is involved in printmaking and mixed media. Behind a closed door is the kitchen where Sesame lives and the adjoining tower where Sesame plays.

Living with two artists, Sesame has unusual and irregular hours, but burning the midnight oil is just fine with her. Like all rabbits she is nosy, and while being a little shy with us at first, her curiosity got the better of her. Under the pretense of coming out to use her litter box, she would leave her refuge behind a large overstuffed chair to see what was going on. She must have used her box at least fifteen times while we were there.

Eventually she didn't need the excuse to come out and fraternize.

Sesame at 6 pounds is a dwarf mini-lop. For toys she has pine cones, a stack of fire wood and shoes. She doesn't like to be picked up but nudges for attention and sits up. She's quite a clever little rabbit, and it was a challenge to keep ahead of her. Before bunny-proofing was completed in the tower, she figured out how to get the door open by wiggling it in such a way that the bolt fell out that was holding the latch.

**NATURAL ENERGY—NATURAL RESOURCES**
Wood provides fuel for the heater and for Sesame's chewing needs *below*. For a better taste treat, Donna gives her a slice of banana *opposite*.

# "If we can only come to see and embrace nature, we may yet perceive ourselves."

**VISUAL REALITIES**
What does the gentle little lop at Ron's feet *above* have in common with the vigorous rabbits of his paintings? Integrity. All are natural products of the environments that created them.

Sesame was originally purchased as a birthday gift for Ron. After observing the animal and wildlife theme running through a series of Ron's paintings, Donna saw an appreciation for the vitality present in these spirited creatures and knew that Ron would enjoy the additional energy of a rabbit in their daily lives.

## ANIMAL NATURE

*I am an oil painter, and my imagery deals primarily with conflicts which arise due to man's misunderstandings of nature.*

*To me nature is everything, and except for philosophical debate can there be, or should there be true distinction between "humanness" and "animalness?"*

*Regarding the differences however, I define animal nature as a perfectly un-selfconscious state of being in which action, reaction and rest also describe the essence of life. Human nature on the other hand holds that we are separate from nature and invent attitudes to qualify our environment.*

*Resultantly we may be more the animal than animals. The ways in which we view animals surely tell us how we view one another—as we regard animals' cuteness, meekness, worthlessness, stupidity, and viciousness, we regard one another.*

*Animals, I believe, don't give such qualifiers any thought but exist simply and appear to me (without man's intervention) to work well as a part of nature.*

*If we can only come to see and embrace nature we may yet perceive ourselves.*
                    *Ron Westman*

Ron Westman, *Tsunami*, 1984, oil on canvas, 66 x 72″ (photo by the artist)

# Sandy & Muffin: *Shining adaptations*

HOUSE RABBIT OWNERS love to talk about their rabbits. I was discussing mine at great length in a pet store when I was introduced to Dena Sharp, who told me about Sandy, her wonderful white mini-lop. She was so pleased with Sandy that she wanted another house rabbit and was interested in breeding her. I knew that arrangements could be made with Patrick, a gold mini-lop who was staying with us at the time. Now Dena and her husband, Bob, are proud owners of two beautiful white mini-lops.

What's most interesting to me about these rabbits is that they are as far from "natural" as rabbits can get. Yet, with the bond of trust and caring they have with their owners, it works. They have completely adapted to human living. They fit in with what their owners do and go where their owners go. It may be just a weekend trip or it may be across country. Sandy has done extensive car traveling (described on page 106).

**BUNNY BATHS**

Dena's pride and joys, these rabbits are doted upon, groomed, and even bathed in the kitchen sink. Dena has bathed Sandy all of her life and has started Muffin already (at four months old). She bathes them less frequently in the winter, and never at the same time because the drying procedure is too long. After she rubs them dry with a towel, they lick themselves and give their coats a sheen.

Having no fear of water, they are graceful swimmers, who go on vacations and show off at a nearby lake.

Neither mother nor daughter is the least bit timid. Sandy was raised in the bathroom without a cage, and her daughter has followed suit. They both sleep there at night and when Dena is away at work. For any chewing problems, Dena has found that Cat Away is obnoxious to her rabbits. They also respond to verbal discipline and understand a few words.

We had met several house rabbits with cat or dog friends, but not a bird friend. Dena told us of an amusing incident when Dizzy, her new parakeet came to live with them. Dizzy wanted a friend and decided a baby bunny would do. He ran around Muffin and groomed her, Muffin responded to this display of affection the way a house rabbit should. The rabbit licked the bird.

Perhaps a friendly rabbit will accept friendship from any source that offers it.

## LIKE MOTHER LIKE DAUGHTER
Dena sees a few differences in her mother/daughter team, but both are mellow. Sandy *inset* is the originator of the family rabbit interest.

Photo *inset* by Bob Sharp

# Abigail: *Priceless entertainment*

HER SHOW OF AFFECTION and her playfulness are what Lori Peterson and her husband, Randy Chafe, like most about Abigail, their mini-lop. As she follows them around, she rubs her nose against them, licks them and entertains them. She has racing paths through the living room, where she runs, jumps, and spins around in midair.

Abigail has never been caged and can be considered unlimited except for the gate across the bedroom door. Running loose in the living room and kitchen, she is very unusual in not bothering the mass of exposed electrical cords.

Abigail has been raised with rather strict discipline, which she has responded to with surprising intelligence. She knows she is not supposed to be on the furniture but tries to get away with what she can. When the Chafes come home from work, they may find her lounging in a chair, which she quickly vacates as they come in the door.

Her housebreaking was accomplished by persistently putting her in the litter

box and reprimanding her for her mistakes. For the few "stragglers" that are common even for the most conscientious house rabbits, Lori uses a dustbuster (a small portable vacuum cleaner).

Lori and Randy have proved something valuable to owners of rabbits with crooked teeth (a malady explained on page 93). A pet does not have to be disposed of for this physical defect. They have her teeth clipped once a month by her veterinarian at a very reasonable cost. Abigail is worth every penny of her maintenance, and considering other forms of entertainment, Abigail is a real bargain.

**A HARDWORKING HOUSE MATE**
Abigail earns her keep by working for her treats *above*. She also helps out around the house by removing the newspapers *opposite*.

# Dritzel: *A man's best friend*

FEW RABBITS COULD boast of a better life than Dritzel, a three-pound Dutch dwarf, who lives with his human companion, Michael Bass, in a San Francisco house. Dritzel has complete freedom of the house, a large sundeck in the back, and a securely fenced yard a few steps down from the sun deck.

He goes in and out as he pleases but often prefers to sleep in the wooden house that Michael has built for him on the deck.

Dritzel may be a little suspicious of strangers intruding in his rabbit utopia, but he is extremely affectionate and trusting with Michael. "One-owner-rabbits" are less common than "one-owner-dogs," but the loyalty is just as easy to recognize.

We could see while we were there how fondly Dritzel licked Michael's neck as he was being held, and it was obvious that there was a close relationship. Dritzel made no effort to get down but was content to be held indefinitely.

We had to laugh when Michael told us of the events that led up to his acquiring a rabbit. He said he had wanted one as a child and was sure he was going to get one when he was told that his mother was going away, and when she came back, she would have a big surprise for him. He picked the name of Mopsy for his new rabbit, and when she returned with his new baby sister, Mopsy became his sister's nickname.

Michael didn't get his rabbit until years later when he was approached by a woman in a parking lot with a boxful of bunnies. On an impulse, Michael took one home and then decided to wait for his rabbit to display his characteristics before naming him.

As it turned out, Dritzel was the name

**EXAMINATION OF THE EVIDENCE**
Dritzel leans forward to smell and listen before judging strangers, but he runs to Michael's arms without reservation.

Michael built Dritzel's house on the deck just next to the living room door. It provides shelter whenever Dritzel wants to be outside.

of a fictitious character in a story Michael told to children. This character was very good-natured and playful but took things he did too far and wound up in all kinds of mischief.

One day when Michael was cleaning his rabbit's playhouse, the rabbit decided to help by pulling his litter box into his house while Michael was trying to pull it out, by pulling the newspaper back under the house while Michael was trying to pull it out, and finally by playing a little tug-of-war with his little piece of carpet. At this point, Michael was reminded of the Dritzel in the children's story and decided that would be his rabbit's name.

# "Dritzel had been trying to say something about water for a day and a half."

Michael told us that Dritzel follows him around the living room, into the kitchen and, yes, even to the bathroom. His favorite game is to run circles around Michael's feet and in between his legs while "honking" and "purring." Michael says the circles get wider and wider as Dritzel runs faster and faster. Then he finally comes up to Michael and stands on his hind feet as if he wants to speak.

Michael tries to listen if he thinks Dritzel is really trying to tell him something. Several years ago Dritzel kept going into the bathroom and circling the toilet. Michael thought it was just a new game until he started eating the potted plants voraciously and even pulled one over. Michael decided something was wrong. When he checked Dritzel's water bottle he found it full, but no water was coming out. The one-way valve was stuck. Dritzel had been trying to say something about water for a day and a half.

A delightful routine is their "dining" together. Dritzel likes to investigate whatever Michael is doing and eat at the same time Michael is eating. Sometimes when Michael is eating dinner, Dritzel will go out to his house on the sun deck and bring in a carrot. He then sits down

**PROVISIONS IN THE PANTRY**
Just off the kitchen is Dritzel's indoor litter box which is no more obtrusive than a waste basket in the corner.

and eats his carrot under the dining table.

Dritzel also comes and sits under the kitchen table when Michael is studying, or he will come into the living room and stretch out next to whatever chair Michael is sitting in. The story here, Michael says, is that "Rabbits, too, are man's best friends."

# Patrick: *The college roommate*

AN EIGHT-POUND arrogant tortoise-marked golden lop, Patrick is a rabbit who gets around a lot. He takes weekend car trips with his roommate, Beth Woolbright, as well as round trips to Texas by plane. He has been a guest in many homes (including ours) and has sired a few "children."

At the time I first met Patrick, he and Beth were spending the summer in a Berkeley apartment. With the cage door open at all times, Patrick has complete freedom wherever he takes up residence. His cage is used only as a feeding and resting area when *he* chooses.

Living in this particular third-floor apartment, Beth would open the front door and allow Patrick additional freedom to run up and down the hall of the apartment building. While I was there Patrick was joined by a neighbor cat. After a few minute's romp, Patrick came shooting in the front door and headed straight to the bedroom. He jumped into his cage, urinated, then jumped out again and went back out to play. I thought this was remarkably good behavior.

Patrick's favorite toys are cardboard boxes and a large rubber ball. His favorite treats are bananas (peels and all) and

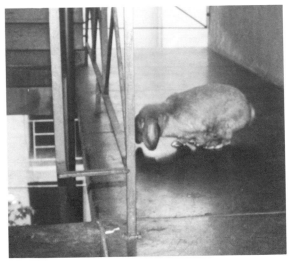

soda crackers, which he will grab from a hand with astonishing speed.

Being quite opinionated he may get angry enough to go into Beth's closet and toss her shoes around. Beth says Patrick knows when he's being manipulated. He may follow the apple she's holding in front of him to coax him out of a room, but then to show he's still in charge, he turns his back on her until she sets the apple on the floor. I've seen him go

**THIRD FLOOR PLAYGROUND**
Beth waits with Patrick for playmate Sam to come through the open front door *opposite*. Their play area includes the entire outside hall *above*.

# "...this long-eared roommate has often proved to be a mighty large distraction."

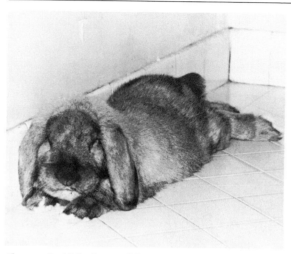

through this incredible face-saving routine, in my house. Pretending it's unimportant, he will turn his back on something he wants!

Patrick's intelligence was "tested" at a pre-school where Beth worked. He was to run through a maze to a reward. Patrick confidently jumped over the maze. Wasn't it obvious that the shortest distance between two points is a straight line?

During Beth's last semester in her college dormitory, Patrick was discovered and evicted. He stayed with us until after graduation, and we learned a lot from him to say the least.

## RABBITS AS ENTERTAINMENT

*One of the by-products, I've decided, about sharing a room with a free-running rabbit is that this long-eared roommate has often proved to be a mighty large distraction. For one thing, bunnies are so innately cute that they are hard to ignore, but that is especially so when the little critter goes around doing those things in life that just come natural.*

*For instance, there is something very sweet about the way a rabbit washes his face, and who among us can look upon a relaxed rabbit that has "kicked back" on the hearth—slowly slipping into bunny sleep—and yet be able to suppress laughter at the enormous dimensions of a rabbit's hind feet?*

*Whether it's observing bunny disappear into a waste basket only to reappear seconds later with a banana peel snack or seeing him stand up on hind legs to get a better view of the world, pet rabbits are pleasant to watch as they do their thing.*

*Beth Woolbright*

**A COOL HEAD**
Patrick knows where to spend a hot afternoon *above*. A bathroom floor also seems an appropriate place to wash his ears *opposite*.

# The Bun: *A respectable foundling*

ORDINARILY, AN ANIMAL moving into a human residence has to do most of the adjusting. This was not the case for The Bun, a ten-pound white rabbit, when he moved in with Jack Rosenberger. Respecting an animal as an animal, Jack was willing to meet The Bun halfway.

Both made adjustments and developed the most beautifully integrated human/animal lifestyle that we have seen, without losing the integrity of either.

When I first talked to Jack on the phone, I did think it sounded bizarre to have a bale of hay in the living room. When Bob and I went over with our cameras, we thought it looked logical, even downright useful. The bale of hay could serve as a coffee table or a bench or a counter to set things on. The Bun could nibble on it whenever and wherever he pleased. Book cases made of packing crates also seemed logical. The soft wooden crates diverted chewing from the books and were replaceable as they became worn down.

The Bun was never put in a cage but made use of a litter box behind the front door. This is particularly interesting because The Bun was fully grown when he moved in. It appears that rabbits can take to a litter box at any age.

Feeling that The Bun needed his own space, Jack provided him with a burrow. An unused fireplace and a side-turned wicker basket became The Bun's burrow, where he ate and slept.

Along with the use of alternative furniture, a few precautions were taken. Electrical wiring was hidden, and the phone cord was put into a garden hose, before The Bun was given complete free-

Photo by Wrenn Dabney Reed

**COOLING OFF IN THE FIREPLACE**
The big yawn of contentment *opposite* radiates its
own warmth. Friends, rabbit and human, *below*
share a mutually agreeable space.

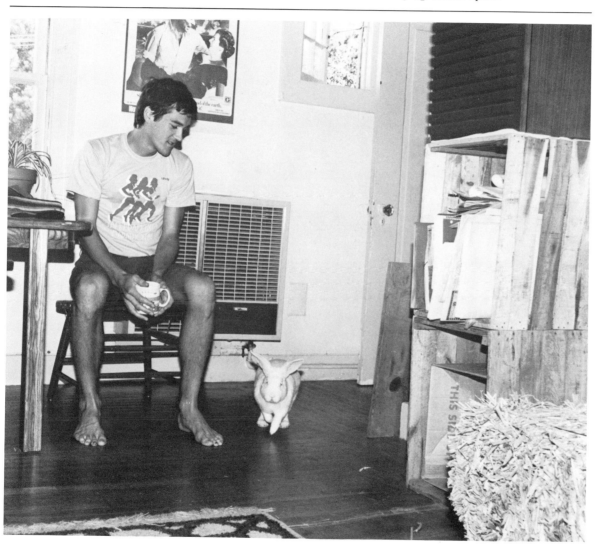

# "We don't feel like we own The Bun. Rather, we are his guardians."

dom of the apartment.

By the time we met The Bun he exuded total confidence in his environment and the people in it. He greeted us with cordial licking and lap hopping as we sat with him on the floor. When he was ready for exercise, he scratched on the front door and was let out into the hall.

Jack took us for a walk around the neighborhood and showed us The Bun's play yards. Being a vegetarian himself, Jack felt that The Bun should have access to his own kind of natural foods. Jack had obtained permission from several neighbors to exercise and graze his rabbit in their yards once or twice a week. He supervised the activity so that only the "right" plants were eaten (which to the yard owners were largely weeds).

It's no wonder The Bun had developed a sense of self-importance. He seemed to realize his own intrinsic value, not for having been purchased at a great price, as one of an exotic breed, but rather for being just a refreshingly ordinary, marvelous, healthy white rabbit.

**AFTER A CARROT, SAMPLE THE SOFA**
It's all right for The Bun to nibble on this bale of furniture. Later this house rabbit will graze and exercise in various friendly backyards.

**RABBIT NON-OWNERSHIP**

*Late one night when Wrenn was driving home she saw a large white rabbit run across the street and hide beneath a parked car. She stopped her car, which is also a rabbit, although blue, and grabbed the rabbit and brought it home. That was two years ago.*

*Initially we tried to find his "owners," but we couldn't. Then we thought about keeping him. Our landlord didn't object, and we quickly fell in love with The Bun, although now I realize it's the other way around; he seduced us.*

*Neither Wrenn nor I would ever go to a pet store and buy a rabbit. We don't feel like we "own" The Bun. Rather we are his guardians. A domestic rabbit like The Bun couldn't have survived outdoors for very long, so our living room became his home. In it can be found several small trees, a variety of logs, stumps, and branches, and where there once was a couch, there is now a fifty-pound bale of hay. Granted it looks peculiar at first, but it's the best arrangement for all of us, and one which I hope lasts a very long time.*

*Jack Rosenberger*

# Herman: *The house supervisor*

BARGING INTO OUR lives uninvited, Herman changed everything we ever thought about rabbits. With a manner that was smug and complacent and intelligence that rivaled a dog's, she took over our house and never gave it back.

Herman spent two years with us before a rare appendix problem took her life. We wish it could have been longer, but the pleasure she gave us in those two years is still with us.

As you may have guessed, we thought she was a he when we first found her in the backyard, but by the time we discovered our error, she came when she was called and knew her name as Herman.

Fourteen pleasing pounds at maturity, she was big in every way—size, character, personality and heart. She carried an enormous dewlap under her chin, and one ear sort of lopped. Her legs were too short for her large, stocky body, but so what? To us she was beautiful.

She had the run of the house and access to a small porch but, most of the time, preferred the comfort and luxury of life indoors. She never required a dark, quiet corner for daytime rest but stayed at my feet as I worked in my studio.

Her sense of propriety was startling.

Of course there was only one right way to pick her up, but she also knew how the furniture should be arranged and where things should be placed. This trait made box training a snap. She trained herself even before I knew it was possible to housebreak a rabbit. She found a good place for her litter box under the kitchen window. This was very convenient for me. With a Pooper Scooper, I could toss the droppings out the window into the vegetable garden below.

She was confined to the kitchen at first but gradually took on the whole house. For chewing control we did a bunny-proofing job on our house and offered plenty of alternatives (pages 82–85). We tried to keep her out of our bedroom, but she was very persistent.

By six months old she would sneak into the bedroom and become so exhilarated over her victory that she would turn our bed into a trampoline. We were so amused that we let her have it during the day. We continued to put her in the kitchen at night while she continued to

**THE OVERSEER'S PLATFORM**
Stretched out serenely on the hearth in the middle of the house, Herman is confident that she won't miss a thing.

# "We had to adjust to having our faces licked every ten minutes all through the night."

insist on sleeping with us. It took another six months before she won. We had to adjust to having our faces licked every ten minutes all through the night. It did occur to me to turn over, but I'd usually find that she was standing on my hair and had me pinned to the pillow. We finally got used to it. To any accusation that Bob and I have something missing in our relationship with each other, I can only say that Herman always moved herself discreetly to the foot of the bed at the appropriate times. She was no dumb bunny.

## KEEPING SCORE

Her propriety showed in fairness to Bob. When it was the correct time for him to pet her, she would lick his hand then shove her head under it. I can't claim she counted, but after a given number of strokes, it was her turn to lick him again.

In seeing that things were properly done, she supervised all household activities, whether it was fixing the washer or sorting out magazines, and left the distinct impression of evaluating all.

Propriety could also be mixed with playfulness, as she would grab a magazine or newspaper out of our hands and run off with it. After a few times chasing her around the room we realized it was the attention she wanted, not the paper, and she knew how to get what she wanted. "You cheat," I often told her. "You manipulate me with your charms, and it's not fair!"

At times she was downright sneaky, but her guilt was revealed by her tail. I could walk by her without realizing that she had pulled a book out of the bookcase, until I saw her tail switching defiantly.

Some behavior may never be explained. One incident involved our cat, Nice, who was engaged in the not-so-nice activity of torturing a mouse. She would turn the mouse loose and let it almost get away, then pounce on it just before it was out of sight. Herman observed this demonstration and thumped her foot in protest. When the protest was ignored, Herman attacked the cat from behind and knocked her off her feet, allowing the mouse to escape. I had mixed emotions over the episode. A minute before, I was pitying the mouse. Now I was concerned over it being loose in the house. Then I pitied Nice for not knowing what on earth had provoked

**SHARING?—WELL, SOMETIMES**
Competing with Nice for the same lap *top left*,
Herman is unchallenged in her claim to the vegetable
drawer *top right*. She enjoys sharing naps on human
beds with humans *bottom*.

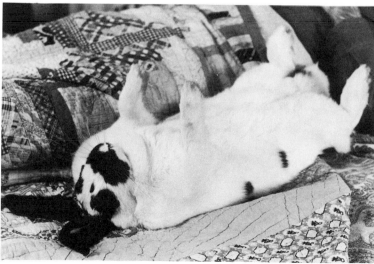

that attack from Herman. Then I began to wonder what had gone on in Herman's little head. Why had she protected a mouse? Do animals preyed upon feel an alliance against predators? This is something I will probably never know.

The whole family used Herman for stress reduction, and at times I even questioned the idea of pets being child substitutes. Sometimes our roles were switched, and she was a parent (or grandparent). She didn't really wipe away tears with her apron, but she could certainly soothe and comfort us and assure us that things were okay.

Having her with me at all times in my home office/studio seemed the natural way to conduct my business. She had added such a new dimension to my life that I felt I had grown an extra limb. When I lost her, I may have been less of a freak, but I felt like an amputee.

I must confess also to a psychological bondage. We took her with us in our heads to many places where one would not expect to find a rabbit. A dinner-party guest, seated next to one of us, was usually unprepared for the conversation. "Oh, you haven't heard of our wonderful rabbit? Well, let me tell you . . ."

## OWNERS SPEAK OUT

Most house rabbit owners (or guardians) have a compulsion to talk about their rabbits. But I think most of us can be forgiven for wanting to tell all, because rabbits have for so long been mislabeled, misunderstood and underrated as pets.

The house rabbit owners participating in this book are hoping that their combined efforts will encourage many other people to find equally marvelous experiences with house rabbits in their own homes.

Our aim throughout this section has been to show you by these examples that rabbits *can* live with people and to show you the products of these situations.

Instead of listing arguments for and against rooming with a rabbit, we have chosen to let these examples speak for themselves.

With some examples we've emphasized personality, with others, methodology and environment. The purpose was to give a sampling of what is *possible* and what others have done.

The rest is up to you.

# PART III:
# STEPPING INTO THE OWNER'S SHOES

IF YOU FEEL you can no longer live without a house rabbit, you will want to know how you can live *with* a house rabbit. Most of us who have been through the process of training our rabbits (and ourselves) have groped for answers. We had no one to turn to for advice. Books on so-called "pet" rabbits gave us recipes and pelting procedures, not house-breaking techniques or chewing-control methods.

House rabbit owners feel less alone now that we can all recognize one another. Having been duly initiated, we proudly wear the labels of our rabbits. Our belts, purse straps and shoelaces are somewhat frayed, and the corners of our briefcases bear similar marks of distinction.

To join this select society you are required to have a sense of humor. It will help you through times of vexation. The other times you will handle with common sense, instinct and what you have learned from other rabbit owners.

This section relies on the expertise of veteran house-rabbit owners and deals with "how to."

Photo by Amy Shapiro

# The Nitty-Gritty of Toilet Training

THE FIRST MATTER of concern to people with any house pet is "toilet training." Rabbit feces are not as "potent" as that of dogs or cats, and a few hard odorless droppings are just a nuisance rather than a major disaster. Urine, which can damage floors and furniture, is much more important to control. The rules you follow for training will depend on whether you plan to use a cage alone, a cage and a litter box or just a litter box.

All three ways start with confinement until the right habit is formed, followed by freedom as it is earned.

Photo by Amy Shapiro

Most rooms have a corner. You can put the litter box in the corner and show bunny where it is, repeatedly. If you're flexible, bunny can pick his own spot, and results will be much faster. Even in a cage, rabbits often show a preference for the back corner away from their door.

Physical reminders will be necessary at first, especially for very young rabbits. You will supervise his freedom and carry him back frequently to the box or cage. Some will learn the word "box" and run to it when they're reminded verbally.

If a "memory lapse" results in a wet rug, blot it thoroughly with a dry tissue or rag then sponge it up with warm water. A little ammonia or Lysol will remove any remaining odor.

Unless you can watch closely, it's advisable to keep bunny off the beds and upholstered furniture until a box habit is well established. A soft cushion may feel too much like soft litter material.

### SUGAR COATING THE PILL

Sooner or later you can expect reasonable urine control from your house rabbit. "Pill" control is not as easy to achieve for some and depends largely on individual metabolism. A few rabbits drop pills only while they're eating. For this reason even an uncaged rabbit can be fed in a cage, and some are fed next to or in the litter box itself. Others may drop pills only while they're sleeping, and they can be confined during naps.

The best behaved house rabbits are the ones that will sit for long periods of time on the litter box (or in the cage) and try to get everything done at once. They often take care of their grooming at the same time. Having a rabbit like this is largely due to luck, but you can do a few things to encourage this habit: (1) make the litter box a pleasant place and don't use it for punishment, (2) praise and pet him when he's done well, (3) maintain a fairly regular feeding and snack routine, and (4) keep stray pills picked up so as not to encourage more.

In all honesty I have to admit that some house rabbits can be toilet trained better than others. But you don't have to throw out a less trainable rabbit. You can observe his "cycle," or the times of day he scatters pills about. You can keep him confined during these times, or you can stand by with the whisk broom. Sweep-up is unlikely to be needed more than twice a day (unless you're expecting company).

# "Every house rabbit owner wants a cage or litter box which is clean and odor-free..."

**CAUSES OF SLIP-UPS**

There are a few occasions in which even the best trained house rabbits may temporarily forsake their good toilet habits. The causes may be (1) illness or extreme anxiety or fear, (2) a need to mark their boundaries during times of insecurity, (3) rebelliousness over being denied something they want, (4) need of attention, (5) sexual excitement, which sometimes causes spraying or the dropping of "identity marbles." This is not so much of a problem with just one house rabbit, but with two or more uncaged house rabbits of opposite sexes, you will have to look into neutering anyway.

**COPING WITH CLEANUP**

Every house rabbit owner wants a cage or litter box which is clean and odor free, with the least amount of effort. Everyone disagrees on which is easiest. Some feel that it's easier to clean out a litter box than a whole cage. Others would rather bypass a litter box altogether and have bunny use just the cage. Still others feel that keeping up both cage and litter box together is easier, since cleanings are less frequent.

Litter boxes come in a number of styles and shapes. I've seen everything from roasting pans and cookie sheets to large sand boxes. What you put in it depends on where it is and what your rabbit does with it. I fall back on cat litter for boxes on rugs. Corn cob bedding is less dusty but costly in small quantities. Pine shavings smell wonderful but are terribly unruly, especially on carpeting. They stick to bunny's feet and get scattered everywhere. Compressed shavings are a little better, and cedar chips are a lot better (but more expensive). My compromise is to put pine shavings or cedar chips into the cage trays, where wire mesh flooring holds them in place, and cat litter into open boxes. Cedar chips are suitable for open boxes in uncarpeted areas, or anywhere that sweepup is easy.

**KEEPING UP WITH THE CAGE**

Cage upkeep usually starts with some sort of absorbent material (pine shavings, cedar chips or cat litter) placed on top of a newspaper lining in the cage tray. For a large rabbit using the cage and an outside litter box, the cage would be changed about twice a week. Without a litter box to share the load, the cage would need to be changed about every other day and for some, every day. If you're relying on

**POPULAR STYLES IN TOILETS**
Daphne finds amusement on her flat tray *left*.
Buns uses a baking dish inside her cage *top right*.
Elliot and Mayo share a large cat box. *lower right*.

newspapers alone, they would certainly need to be removed daily.

Any shavings or litter material on the bottom of the cage tray should not be piled high. The purpose of the wire floor is to let the droppings fall through it and not force your rabbit to lie in his own feces. If the layer of litter material is too thick, the droppings sit on the top where bunny can't get away from them. Many of us get carried away by the nice aroma of the shavings and overdo it.

Wood shavings and rabbit droppings can be dumped directly from the cage into the garden for use as mulch and fertilizer.

If you live in an apartment and have to use a disposal service, here's an easy way to remove litter. Lay a large plastic leaf bag on the floor. Remove the cage tray and slide it completely into the leaf bag. Close the bag around the tray, then turn it over so that the tray dumps its contents into the bag. I change cages like this in my living room with no mess.

**TOOLS OF THE TRADE**

The handy whisk broom is a staple as far as I'm concerned. It can be used for brushing off the cage as well as sweeping up stray litter. I haven't yet invested in a Dustbuster, but that's next on my list. These portable little vacuum cleaners are perfect for keeping stray pills picked up as well as wood shavings, hair or whatever else might get scattered in between regular cleanup days.

Cages that get full time use should be cleaned with a disinfectant about once a month. This can be done with Lysol or any of the pine disinfectants. Disinfecting once every three to four months is enough for cages with part time use.

Good hygiene is a good health practice, but it has its other benefits, too. We've had as many as five full-grown house rabbits (counting boarders) at one time, and usually the first comment visitors make walking into our house is, "Funny, it doesn't smell like rabbit in here."

Well, I don't know what "rabbit" is supposed to smell like, but I do know that under the right conditions any species could generate an odor. If you were to put five humans into small cages over open toilets, how long would you stay in the same room or even in the same yard? Yet we as humans don't think of ourselves as being smelly. Allowed equal hygiene, rabbits are among the least obnoxious smelling animals you'll ever find.

# How to Save Your House

RABBITS MUST CHEW in order to keep their ever-growing teeth filed down, but they *must* be prevented from chewing on the wrong things.

If you want your living room to look as unscathed as Betty Tsubamoto's (above) with a rabbit in it, there are a few measures you will have to take to protect your possessions from your pet and your pet from your possessions. Prevention is usually cheaper than repair, but most house rabbit owners lose a phone cord before they realize this.

Most of us use a combination of discipline, physical prevention and chewing alternatives.

### DISCIPLINE—RABBIT STYLE

Discipline works if you're there to enforce it, but most rabbits can get into mischief when your back is turned. Bunny discipline in most cases is a sharp "No!" (or a clap of the hands or a stomp

# "Chewing on your clothing isn't always with the intention of chewing on you."

of the foot—anything that startles).

If you spend a lot of time at home, gentle but consistent discipline may eventually pay off by conditioning your house rabbit into good behavior.

Most chewing problems have to do with the house not with people, but I will mention people-chewing here because the cure is discipline, and if you're the one being bitten, you're obviously there to enforce the discipline.

It's common for baby rabbits to go through a stage of testing their teeth. If your bunny decides to test his teeth on you, I advise a small screech. (It doesn't have to be a blood-curdling yell). He will understand a shrill squeal and catch on very quickly that he has caused you discomfort. This technique has never failed us, even for our "mean" Phoebe.

Pet rabbits can be misinterpreted. Chewing on your clothing isn't always with the intention of chewing on you. They sometimes pull and tug on fabric to move it out of the way. We had originally thought that Herman was trying to bite our arms when she grabbed at our sleeves. We finally realized that once our sleeves were rolled up, she licked our arms.

## PHYSICAL PREVENTION—BUNNY-PROOFING

Some protection for your house in the way of "bunny-proofing" is almost always necessary for living with uncaged house rabbits. The extent of bunny-proofing will depend entirely on what your individual rabbit goes for. Usually it will be only one or two particular places that I will call "problem areas." The cause can be something as simple as a cookie crumb deep in the carpet that attracts digging or chewing. The smell of damp wood on a rainy day might also stimulate extra chewing.

Not all house rabbits respond the same way and you will certainly not require all of the bunny-proofing material I'm suggesting. This is simply a list, gathered as a collection from my experts (house rabbit owners) of the materials that *can* be used.

1. A small sheet of plexiglass from the hardware store can cover a problem area of linoleum, hardwood floor or even wall. It's transparent, and you can hardly tell it's there.

2. Bitter Apple, Cat Away or Lysol can be sprayed on soft or hard material and will make the object unpalatable to many rabbits. Tobasco sauce on hard surfaces

has been known to discourage chewing in some cases, and our daughter has found some of her favorite perfumes to be positively disgusting to our rabbits.

Parents of small children may be familiar with thumb-sucking remedies, which might also be effective on rabbits. Experimentation will indicate which works best on your rabbit, but I have learned that any deterrent has to be sprayed or rubbed on repeatedly.

Perhaps when the manufacturers of pet products realize our needs, they will come up with an effective, harmless chewing repellant for house rabbits.

3. A thin wooden bumper can save a baseboard. The bumper is just a small strip of untreated wood tacked over a problem area. It not only protects the baseboard but provides a chewing block. If you need a flexible covering, garden aluminum, in 4-inch wide rolls, can be cut with scissors to any length and tacked or stapled over problem areas. (We use this on our wooden porch.

4. Electrical cords can be housed inside garden hose, plumber's pipe or plastic tubing. When I learned about plastic tubing, sold in any hardware store for about 12 cents a foot, I bought a bunch for my computer cords. The tubing can be slit lengthwise, and with the cord shoved inside, the tubing closes right back around the cord. It's easy, and it works. I won't say that it's impossible for a rabbit to chew through it, but it would take a long time and can be replaced before that happens.

5. Phone cords can be run through on-wall plastic casings, complete with elbows (sold also in hardware stores), which have a finished look and do not detract from room decor.

6. There are also ways to hide wiring by furniture arrangement. We have too much furniture stuffed into a small house, and we can stick a piece of furniture or even a waste basket over practically any problem. Needless to say, we buy cheap, unfinished straw waste baskets.

7. For protection against toenails and teeth, a blanket "throw" or a large towel can be tossed over upholstery or beds. These items can take everyday wear and be removed if you're expecting company.

8. An inexpensive grass mat can be laid on top of any frayed section of a more expensive rug. This is a great diversion for cat clawing as well as bunny chewing. and could also be considered a toy.

# "You can find harmless entertainment for your house rabbit..."

## ALTERNATIVES—TOYS

The materials mentioned so far are to prevent chewing. On the other hand, rabbits need harmless chewing materials to keep their teeth in good shape (and consequently to stay alive).

We call these materials alternatives, since they are given in place of forbidden items in your house. They can be considered toys much the same as a dog enjoys a chew toy or a bone. House rabbits appear to derive as much pleasure from their toys, which provide chewing, digging and general entertainment.

For starters, here are a few favorites reported by house rabbit owners:

1. Firewood with bark or any untreated scrap wood, small branches from fruit and fir trees—all help grind down bunny's ever-growing teeth.
2. Paper bags and cardboard boxes serve for crawling inside, scratching around and additional chewing.
3. For digging, a litter box satisfies this need. If digging results in litter all over the floor, a deeper box or one with a hood might be logical. Without a litter box, an old blanket, rug or towel will do (see Charlie, page 19).

For excessive digging needs see page 94.

4. Newsprint paper or paper towels are fun for shredding with teeth or feet, but keep it to a small quantity. Most house rabbits like to play with newspapers. Although printers' ink no longer contains lead, it smears, so unprinted paper is a cleaner, better choice when available.
5. A handful of hay or straw provides harmless chewing pleasure, but keep it on an uncarpeted area. Straw rugs and waste baskets (recommended as prevention devices) are also toys to rabbits.
6. Dog chew-toys that have a cereal or grain base (read the ingredients) are also enjoyed by rabbits.
7. Nudge-and-roll toys can be large rubber balls or cyclinders such as empty salt cartons and toilet paper spools. Also there is a cat toy, a ball made of metal rings, that our rabbits like to pick up with their teeth and throw.
8. Some house rabbits like carry-around toys like a small paper cup or maybe an old shoe (see page 45).

You can find harmless entertainment for your house rabbit that can satisfy just about any chewing or scratching need. Alternatives, along with prevention and discipline, can keep house rabbits safe, happy and enjoyable to their owners.

**THE BEST THINGS IN LIFE ARE ALMOST FREE**
Agarami chews on logs *top left*. Phoebe rolls a salt carton *top right*. Daphne and Ninja hide in a cardboard box and a bag *lower left, right*.

Photo *top left* by Rachael Millan

# Managing Multiples

VERY OFTEN house rabbit owners would like to add a second little pal to their families. This can be very difficult because rabbits don't readily accept newcomers invading their territories. Even if they don't actually fight, they claim and reclaim territory by doing obvious things to leave their scents around. Odors are still more pronounced by courting couples trying to attract each other. In spite of it all, you may still want to add one, and it *can* be done.

We have accumulated some experience with multiple house rabbits in the last few years. I'm sure there are plenty of exceptions, but for general rules, these are the conclusions we have drawn from what we have seen in our house.

1. If you introduce a companion of the same sex, they are likely to fight, and you will need a closed door between them.

2. Mature rabbits of opposite sexes will either fight or mate. A baby female is usually acceptable to a mature male, but a baby male is not always acceptable to a mature female. (see page 24).

3. If a mother raises a daughter, they

will continue to be friendly, and no neutering is necessary.

4. Two sisters raised together make very good companions. (If you know in advance that you want two.)

5. It's possible for a father and son (by blood or adoption) to get along provided the introduction is long before the son is old enough to be a threat and there are no females around by the time he is.

6. Two brothers raised together will be friendly, at least for awhile, without females around. If they become competitive one or both can be neutered.

### PAIRING OFF

I had no plans to discuss breeding, because this book is on pet rabbits not livestock, and there are always problems to face with the casual breeding of pets. My advice is to leave the breeding up to professional breeders, who know what they're doing (although I haven't followed my own advice).

One of the few justifications for breeding pet rabbits is that it's so very difficult to add one otherwise. Sometimes there might be pressure from friends who know *your* rabbit and want one of the offspring. With such temptation it's hard to resist giving it a try.

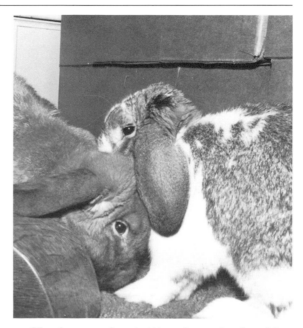

Hygiene and nutritional needs should be met with care during the gestation period of 28–31 days. Most books say that the pregnant doe should be kept quiet and free from stress. But what is stress to a house rabbit, who's used to people talking, stereos playing and phones ringing? Our only difficulty with Daphne was that her sudden weight gain made her very clumsy, and she took some bad falls. Confinement was then necessary for her safety, not for psychological stress.

Photo by Tania Harriman

**BREAKFAST IN BED**
Different from a cat or dog, Daphne stands in
nursing position over her brood, which receives
her rich milk only once a day, or every 20 hours.

Indoors the expectant mother can get by very nicely with a large cage (20″ × 30″ for a rabbit 8 lbs. and up). If it has a top opening at one end, a box of straw or wood shavings can be shoved to the other end, away from the opening where she jumps in and out. As her pregnancy advanced, Daphne wanted to use her litter box outside the cage (apparently to keep her cage clean), and we lifted her in and out to prevent possible injury while jumping.

Daphne's nest box has been used by several other house rabbits and works well for that size cage. The four-inch high box takes up most of the far end of the cage. The box has no bottom because it sits on the wire floor of the cage and has a thick layer of pine shavings in the tray underneath, which can be pulled out and cleaned when the shavings get moist. The nest box itself is filled with shavings, which, mixed with the fur the mother has pulled out, make a soft little blanket.

Baby rabbits born into this environment appear to think of TV sets, phones, washers, dryers and vacuum cleaners as being natural. Mother rabbits, who already live in this environment and so enjoy being stroked by human hands, certainly don't mind these same human hands stroking their newborn babies.

Raising a litter of house rabbits may be fun, but I warn you it's very painful to give them up, even when you know they're going to wonderful homes.

Another source of pain, overlooked by most people, is the plight of the papa. You might think that a stud house rabbit has a great life—well, he has one day of ecstasy, followed by many of frustration. His mate will make it clear that she has no further use for him as she prepares for the arrival of her babies, although she may at times let him sit wistfully beside her.

**SHOWING OFF STITCHES**
Frisky Abigail surprises Lori with an unexpected jump. She shows no lack of spunk for having been spayed only a few days earlier.

### END-ALL OR CURE-ALL

Our careful family planning for the breeding of our pet rabbits was followed by two "accidents." This can happen too easily when rabbits run loose in the house, and someone forgets to close a bedroom door.

After months of worrying constantly about closing doors, it was a great relief when Patrick, our second male boarder, was neutered. (Dinner, our first male boarder, had already moved out.)

For humans, rabbit sexuality can be a real nuisance, since rabbits can reproduce just about any time. It interferes with litter box habits and can cause aggression in otherwise friendly personalities.

With that said, I now suggest the solution—neutering. It may not end all sex for your rabbit, but it does help a lot of the problems connected with it. Patrick has stopped spraying, and yet he's as much "in love" with Daphne as he ever was. He courts her, and I have witnessed their continued sexual activity. I can only conclude that Patrick's sexuality must be centered largely in his brain.

Sexuality in female rabbits is quite varied. Some have very obvious "heat" cycles, while it's barely noticeable in oth-ers. They can come into heat with or without a male. One example of this is Abigail (this page and also 56), who is an "only child" living with no other pets. Lori had her spayed because Abigail's heat cycles were disrupting her good toilet habits, and sexual activity was not going to be available to Abigail anyway.

We can see very different sexual responses in two of Daphne's daughters, who are constantly exposed to the same male. Dinah tries endlessly to seduce Patrick with behavior considered obscene in humans, while Dominique shows only occasional interest in Patrick.

With individuals being so different, I wouldn't say that *all* house rabbits should be neutered. It's simply an option that can allow more freedom and fun, not less.

**CROSS-SPECIES COMPANIONS**

If you want to add a pet without the complications of mating or fighting, a good choice is a companion of another species. There are a number of combinations that work well, but the most common mix is a rabbit with a cat. You can raise them together or introduce a youngster later. It doesn't matter which comes first. You can give a kitten to a fully grown rabbit or a baby bunny to a fully grown cat. Obviously, this last choice would take more caution and would be impossible if your cat hunts larger game than mice.

Our cat Nice was a ten-year-old indoor city cat, when we found Herman at about six weeks old. Nice was curious but had no desire to eat the rabbit and, in a few days, entered a second kittenhood as she and the rabbit became playmates.

We have seen several grown rabbits, of either sex, accept a new kitten. Only a few precautions are necessary. If the cat and rabbit share a litter box, cleanings are frequent.

The right dog can be compatible with a rabbit. What might prohibit a dog/rabbit frolic is the dog's playful but noisy barking. In our house Rags is more of a protector than a playmate, although she is a good lounge mate. During cold weather Rags and Phoebe sleep together in the kitchen. Before Phoebe's time, Rags used to sit under the table with Herman and wait for treats. Fortunately, with different dietary needs, they didn't vie for the same food.

The worst dog-damage to any of our rabbits is getting whapped in the face by an overly zealous tail.

Other agreeable combinations are rabbit/hamster (page 44) and rabbit/bird (page 54). Any additional friendship can be fun for a house rabbit. Companions don't have to actually play together, but being in the same vicinity gives an extra interest to their lives.

**NOT EXACTLY BIRDS OF A FEATHER**
These soul-mates flock together in spite of
their different sizes and shapes.

Photo by Tania Harriman

# Needs of the Flesh and Fur

THINGS YOU CAN do to safeguard the health of your rabbit include feeding, understanding his bodily functions, preventing illnesses and accidents, getting necessary medical treatment, and providing for general comfort needs. With all that going for you, the chances are good that you will enjoy a long lasting relationship with your house rabbit.

### VEGETARIAN CUISINE

Like most animals, rabbits build their confidence in you and in their environment when they're well fed. Their main diet is rabbit pellets, which you can find in any pet store and in some hardware stores and drug stores. Rabbit pellets don't need to be rationed. The bowl can be filled any time you see it empty, but it should be checked at least once a day. We check ours twice a day because the bowls are small.

Bowls and water bottles come in various sizes. Heavy clay bowls are easy to clean and not so easy to tip over. Small bowls have worked out best for us because our baby rabbits would often climb into a larger bowl, urinate, and make the food inedible.

Water bottles that attach to the side of the cage are convenient, but don't get complacent. They need to be checked often. If the caps aren't screwed on just right, they may leak, and sometimes the metal ball in the one-way valve may stick and block the water passage. I've noticed, however, that the newer bottles seem to be better designed. The neck is not perfectly round so the ball doesn't get stuck.

House rabbits who get plenty of exercise are not likely to get fat unless they're overindulged with treats. There are numerous morsels that rabbits enjoy, and variety is beneficial, but quantities should be limited. Many house rabbits get a small handful of oats in the morning and a chunk of carrot with a few greens for a bedtime snack. Treats vary according to individual tastes.

You will be very confused if you listen to all the do's and don't's of what tidbits you can give your rabbit. My suggestion is to let your bunny try any raw vegetable in a very small amount until you see how well it's tolerated. My rabbits can eat anything, including cabbage and cauliflower, but I personally would avoid anything as questionable as rhubarb. Too much of a good thing can also cause problems. Daphne will get diarrhea if I

**A LAB ANIMAL FOR A SCIENTIST?**
Not for this young scientist. Dominique is in no
danger. Our son Bill does lab work with bacteria in
petri dishes, not rabbits.

give her an extra helping of oats. It's so
hard to say no when she begs.

Sweetened foods should be avoided.
Rabbits don't need extra sugar (even
though they love it), and rotten teeth
would be disastrous for an animal with
such chewing needs. Here again it's hard
to refuse when they stand up and beg
for a cookie. House rabbits are really
good at begging (and stealing when your
back is turned).

Most rabbits enjoy vegetables and
fruits, cereals and grains in addition to
their main diet of pellets. Salt should also
be available, but not all rabbits will use
a salt lick. Some will get their salt from
crackers or nuts, and the smoocher types
will lick people.

### THE PHYSICAL DESIGN PLAN

A rabbit's body has some odd features
(when you're used to dogs and cats). It's
no accident that bunnies love to chew.
They have teeth that grow and have to
be kept filed short by chewing. Their
teeth must be in perfect alignment so
that they can grind against each other.
Without this grinding action the teeth
grow unchecked, and eating becomes impossible. Rabbits without perfect "bites"
can have their teeth filed regularly by

veterinarians, or the owners can learn to
do it themselves.

Rabbit peculiarities don't end with
their teeth. It's hard to believe, when
you see a rabbit gnawing on wood, that
he has a digestive tract that is especially
sensitive to poisons or toxins that might
destroy intestinal bacteria. As an immu-
nology student, our son has explained to
us that a rabbit relies heavily on bacteria
in the cecum to break down cellulose.
The cecum is a pouch-like structure at
the junction of the large and small intestines. Since this is so close to the end of
the digestive tract, few nutrients from it

> ## "There are good reasons to take care of your rabbit's external physique other than just for vanity."

can be absorbed. For this reason the cecum packages special little "vitamin pills" of digested cellulose to be re-ingested. A healthy bacterial culture must be maintained in the cecum in order for the rabbit to survive. This is why veterinarians are so careful in administering antibiotics or any medications to pet rabbits that might destroy intestinal bacteria.

### THE VIRTUES OF VANITY

Even non-scientific, non-medical people can understand the importance of keeping up appearances. There are good reasons to take care of your rabbit's external physique other than just for vanity.

If bunny's toenails are too long they leave scratches when jumping off a piece of furniture or a person's lap. Long toenails may also get caught in the carpeting and damage both rabbit and rug. You can clip the toenails yourself with a grooming kit from the pet store or have it done professionally. Many pet stores will do it for you very inexpensively.

It's hardly worth making a special trip to the veterinarian just for toenails, but if it's combined with other ongoing routine maintenance, your veterinarian will probably be quite reasonable too. I'll mention Abigail again (page 56), who sees her veterinarian, Dr. Donald Griffen, once every month or two for routine teeth and toenail clipping.

### NATURE'S GROOMING KIT

There's another way to keep bunny's toenails short. You can provide him with the opportunity to dig. If you live in a city apartment, you can put a harness and leash on him once or twice a week and take him to the nearest park to scratch around a little.

I have not been able to decide if digging, for a rabbit, is a physical or a psychological need. I was ready at one time to deny that the need really existed. Having lived with sixteen different house rabbits (including offspring and boarders) for months at a time, I was convinced that any digging need could be met indoors for any rabbit. Then along came Dominique, a well behaved house rabbit in every way, except for an excessive digging need that I had not seen in any rabbit before.

Defending my carpet, I put a leash on her and took her outside for a half hour. It worked. By taking her out every second day, I have saved the rug, and she's quite satisfied.

This option is available if you have a house rabbit with excessive digging needs and no access to a secure backyard. It's less demanding than walking a dog twice a day, every day, and you might even enjoy watching your bunny play. You can consider it toenail grooming, healthful exercise or a mental gratification, but it's no more effort than other forms of maintenance.

A word of advice on leashes is to use a light chain type, which cannot be chewed through and watch that it doesn't tangle around small shrubs or bunny's feet.

## CARE OF THE COAT

Grooming and brushing your rabbit's coat is not so much for aesthetics as it is for prevention of hair balls. Rabbits lick themselves as much or more than cats and are subject to the same swallowing of hair. A small wad of Vaseline helps move the hair through the stomach. You don't have to shove it down your rabbit's throat. A dab on his front paws will be licked right off. (A neat trick, huh?) That was a veterinary tip.

Cats and rabbits have similar licking habits, and I've been told by several authorities that cat flea powders are safe to use on rabbits, but flea collars should never be put on a rabbit. I personally don't like using powders either. I keep flea collars on the dog and cat while tediously hand picking the fleas from the rabbits. Jack Rosenberger (page 66) has informed us of an herbal flea powder by Ecosafe Laboratories in Oakland.

All of these tips could be classified as upkeep, beyond which, we are talking about medical problems.

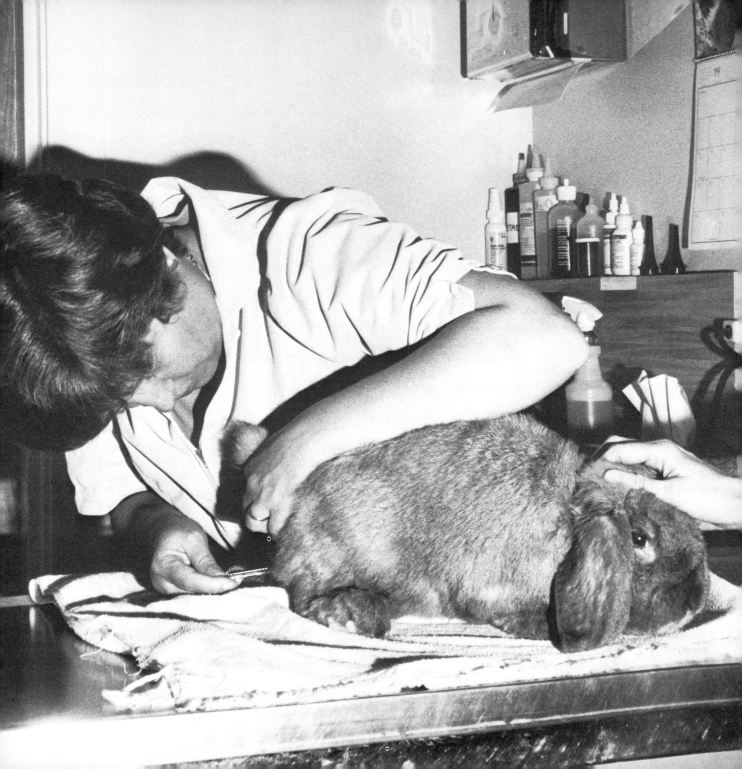

# Professional Pointers—Veterinarian

WHEN IT COMES to treatment of illness and injury other than minor first-aid, we turn to professionals, and although there are no rabbit vaccines, I recommend a thorough checkup for any new bunny.

Many more veterinarians now treat rabbits with the same care as dogs and cats and some have become quite familiar with the eccentricities of rabbits. Among them is Dr. Donald Griffen, who has been very helpful in explaining their special biological functions to us, and Dr. Marliss Geissler, who is familiar with the needs of *house* rabbits.

Since living in a human house is much different from living in a rabbit hutch, there are some unexpected dangers. A cruel fact of life is that with additional freedom there are additional hazards.

For general pointers on what every house rabbit owner should know, we consulted Dr. Marliss Geissler of the Bay Area Pet Hospital. Dr. Geissler knows rabbits as we do—as house pets—and has lived with them herself. I asked her the questions most rabbit owners ask.

### THE BOTTOM LINE
Examined the same as cats and dogs, rabbits are not spared the indignities of the thermometer for revealing illnesses.

### HOME HAZARDS
The first question was "Are there any known house plants that are dangerous for rabbits to chew?"

"Philodendron and English ivy," she told me. This surprised me since I've seen many rabbits chew on these plants.

"Quantities make a big difference," she explained. "If a rabbit ate enough of these plants it could be harmful, but one plant to avoid entirely is dieffenbachia."

Dr. Geissler was not as concerned over house plants as she was over electrical wiring, which is a major cause of accidental death for house rabbits.

Another potential hazard that likely exists in your home, especially if you subscribe to a newspaper, is that harmless looking rubber band. We learned this the hard way in losing one of our rabbits during this writing.

Dr. Geissler said that rabbits can and do pass rubber bands—sometimes, but not always. If you see your rabbit consume a rubber band or a similar non-edible, give him a wad of Vaseline or Laxotone or Petromalt to work it through the digestive tract, then check to see that it passes in the next few days. If it remains in the stomach or intestines it can become life threatening. Rubber bands do not show up on X-rays. "The frustrating thing," Dr. Geissler said, "is that there's no way to test for them."

An autopsy on our rabbit revealed that rubber bands had lodged in her stomach and accumulated hair but caused no blockage. We guessed that they had been there a long time, because the rubber bands on our newspapers had switched from green to red at least two months prior. Those found in her stomach were green. Had they moved into the intestine and caused a blockage, there would have been signs of illness, and a blockage could have been felt upon examination.

We had not seen our rabbit swallow the rubber bands. She seemed healthy, except for occasional diarrhea during her last months while a pathogenic bacteria strain was accumulating in her stomach. She never acted sick until just twenty-four hours before she died of what was probably toxic shock.

I wonder how many rabbit owners have had similar losses without ever knowing what went wrong. The point is, What do we do to avoid this kind of grief? Obviously we should keep these potential killers off the floor and out of bunny's reach. But I think we have all been careless at times due to simple ignorance.

In addition to man-made objects, rabbits carry around their own possible hazards—their own fur. They lick and groom constantly, and Dr. Geissler says that fur balls can be a real problem for rabbits. They don't vomit like cats to get rid of them, and accumulated hair can cause intestinal blockages. Hair balls can be prevented and treated with Vaseline.

## HEALTH IN THE HOUSE

Being interested in promoting health as well as avoiding house hazards, my next question for Dr. Geissler was, "Can rabbits stay healthy without ever going outside?"

"Yes," she told me. "Like cats, they can live healthy lives indoors. However, it's a good idea to open a window to sun light" (not direct sun rays).

Many people believe that any vitamins from the sun are in the rays, but she explained that the existing vitamins are changed by the light into a usable form.

Another suggestion for furthering the good health of an indoor rabbit was a supplement of vitamin D3 (in small quantities). This she said would normally be included in multi-vitamin supplements.

# "Rabbits are now given the same in-depth examinations and, just like other animals, can be treated."

## WHAT TO WATCH

I had already learned that a major barometer of good health in a rabbit is a hearty appetite. What I wanted to know was, "How long should my rabbit (or any rabbit) be off her food before I consult a veterinarian?"

"Not more than 24 hours," Dr. Geissler advised. "With a rabbit's high energy requirements, a prolonged loss of appetite can mean something is seriously wrong.

Other signs of trouble," she said, "are diarrhea with mucous (mucoid enteritis) and runny eyes and nose (snuffles). Both of these are serious illnesses for rabbits, and should be treated promptly."

Rabbits can also be vulnerable to middle ear infections. "The symptoms to watch for here," she said, "are severe head tilts and disorientation."

## TREATMENT

Rabbit infections, Dr. Geissler pointed out, are somewhat tricky to deal with because they are treated with antibiotics, and many antibiotics can throw off the intestinal bacteria balance that a rabbit has to maintain.

This was something that had also been pointed out by Dr. Griffen, and both favor injections, when possible, over oral antibiotics, which have to pass through the digestive tract.

Several rabbit owners have mentioned that their veterinarians advised feeding yogurt or acidophilus after an infection to build up "good" intestinal bacteria.

In preventing external infections in our rabbits, I work on even the slightest scratch with antibiotic ointment. I've been surprised too many times by a small wound that scabs over on the outside hiding the infection underneath.

What we do at home is preventative, but when it comes to a real problem, we get medical treatment for our rabbits.

"We can look for symptoms as we would in any other animal," Dr. Geissler said. "Rabbits are now given the same in-depth examinations and, just like other animals, can be treated."

She reminded us of the time that cats weren't considered worth treating. Now pet rabbits are emerging from the same position, and they too are on their way to being recognized as worthy pets with something to offer.

How long can we hope for these worthy pets to be with us? Our authorities say seven to eight years if all goes well.

# Professional Pointers—Breeder

AN EXPERT ON sustaining the health of numerous rabbits is Carol Babington, owner of a French lop rabbitry. Carol, unlike many professional show-rabbit breeders, does not cull (a euphemism for kill) her rabbits that don't meet show standards. She places her healthy "pet" rabbits in good homes as carefully as she does her "show" rabbits.

Knowing this in advance, we were delighted to visit Carol's rabbitry and learn everything we could from her experience. Her rabbits live in large, beautifully maintained hutches that are actually part of the garden with fenced-in runs, shrubs, fruit trees and lawns.

The idea of a rabbit in the house is nothing new to Carol either. She may bring in one or two at a time (but not the whole rabbitry). Her advice on health care would apply to both indoor and outdoor rabbits.

### CLEAN IS CARING

Her general recommendations are, of course, to keep the cage clean and to maintain a stable environment. When grooming your rabbit you should look for signs of sore hocks on the bottoms of the feet and hutch burn, an inflammation of the urinary area. If you do your own rab-bit's nail clipping, be sure to clip only the clear area, not where any color shows in the nail.

She said to refrain from abrupt changes in the diet and mentioned that the pellets can get moldy and should not sit out for any great length of time. (This would be especially true if the air is moist.) Mold, she told us, can even kill a rabbit. She discards any pellets left in the bowl each day.

Also she advises against putting rugs or blankets inside cages, especially of young rabbits, since the chewing of these items could cause intestinal blockage.

### HEAT BEATERS

Most of us are aware that rabbits can take a lot more cold than heat. House rabbits are seldom exposed to extremes in temperature, but Carol's cooling methods would be useful if the temperature gets unusually high even in the house. She says to fill a gallon milk carton with water and freeze it. Place the frozen container in the cage, and the melting ice will act as an air cooler.

Her other method is one we have used ourselves traveling with our rabbits in hot weather without air-conditioning in our car. Wet towels can be draped over

**ONLY FOR SHOW?**
Instead of being "put down" after losing his right
eye, Carol's handsome ex-show rabbit Sunday is
given extra privileges and anything he wants.

# "Carol has enough accumulated knowledge to write her own book, a concise health guide."

the top and one or two sides of the cage, and the wind blowing through the wet towels will form an evaporative cooler.

I have to add one more. For an uncaged house rabbit, a cool floor (tile, brick, linoleum, etc.) is a belly-cooling aid, and a wet newspaper spread flat on the floor can give additional relief.

Symptoms of heat prostration, Carol told us, include rapid breathing, wetness around the nose and mouth and possibly slight bleeding from the nose.

## APPRAISING PROBLEMS

Carol has a list of health problems for rabbit owners to check. The first one she has listed is diarrhea, which if left untreated, can result in death from dehydration. It is usually caused by stress, abrupt diet change or an intestinal bacteria called coccidiosis.

If diarrhea is severe or persistent, she says to call a vet. The usual medication is Albon, a drug that works very well.

Carol advises checking the ears periodically for a brownish waxy build up that could mean ear mites. This she says is different from the plain wax in ears. With Carol's experience, she takes care of this problem herself. If you suspect mites in your rabbit's ears, you will need to have a veterinarian check them and give you specific medical instructions.

Another kind of mite problem that Carol discussed is skin mite, which is detected by persistent scratching on the middle of the shoulders, sometimes leaving a bald spot. For this she says to use a bird mite spray on the area about once a week for a couple of weeks.

Carol lances and cleans her rabbits' abscesses, which may be caused by sore hocks, punctures or bites. She said that rabbit abscesses do not drain of their own accord like a cat's, and cleaning out the hard pus with a Q-tip and disinfectant is needed daily until it clears up.

For eye infections she loosens any hardened crust with a cotton ball soaked in a 10% boric acid solution, then applies Mycitracin ointment.

Carol speaks from experience with a large number of rabbits. Unfortunately, we can include only a portion of information Carol has to offer. She and Dr. Geissler have worked together formulating health practices and procedures for rabbits, and Carol has enough accumulated knowledge to write her own book, a concise health guide (and I hope she does, for all of us).

# Upward Mobility

YOU WOULDN'T WANT to go to all the loving care of your house rabbit and see that his good health is assured, only to lose him in some mindless accident.

Bunny proofing a house can prevent many accidents, but a possible cause of serious injury is a human—in picking up bunny "wrong." The wrong way is any way that causes him to wrench his back or to kick violently and leave nasty gashes in a person's arm.

Since children are more inclined to want to pick up their pets, it's especially important to teach them *how* right from the start. Yet children can become very competent at lifting rabbits, and I've seen several that could give lessons to adults.

Most rabbit books will say to pick up a rabbit by the scruff on the shoulders. This seems to me too much of a livestock approach and even inhumane for very large rabbits. Most house rabbit owners, that I've met, pick up their rabbits under the shoulders with one hand while supporting the bottom with the other. This works for any size rabbit. After being picked up, however, some would rather be carried in one arm just over the hip.

**IN GOOD HANDS**
Kevin Holmes has experience with rabbits and knows where to put his hands. One hand supports the bottom while the other supports the shoulders.

**EASY LIFT-OFF**
Even a fourteen-pounder can be quite managable
with the two-handed method, at shoulders and
rump. A little practice gives the "feel" of it.

 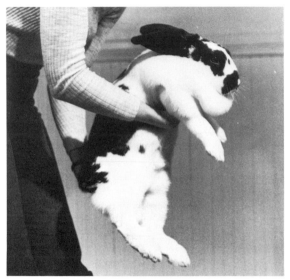

My own technique is to come up behind
my rabbits and swoop them up before
they have time to object. That's why I
was so amazed at Johanna's (page 31)
slow and gentle technique at picking up
Lullabye from the front! I had never seen
this done before and with such ease.

It was mentioned to me recently by
Dena (page 54) that, while her rabbits
can be picked up and held, they don't like
the transition of down to up or up to
down. I've noticed this too, and it appears that even rabbits who like to be
picked up don't particularly like to have
their balance thrown off in the transition.
From what I've seen (and lifted), the
size of a rabbit makes no difference in
willingness to be picked up.

Whatever style you develop in picking
up your own rabbit will seem the only
right way as far as your rabbit is
concerned. If you get one that doesn't
like to be picked up at all, don't think you
have a dud. There are quite a few dogs
in this world that don't like to be picked
up and carried around either. Lifting
your rabbit with ease may simply take
time and practice.

# Outward Mobility

Now that you have bunny picked up, how do you carry him around? That depends on how far you're going. If it's just into the next room, your arms will do, but if you're going across town or across the country, you will need some sort of carrier. Kennel Cabs make good carriers for most purposes. They're convenient to handle and sturdy enough to offer some protection. The ventilation holes are on the sides, not on top. This is preferable for rabbits, because they seem to feel more secure with a solid "roof" over their heads. Carriers are useful for just about any mode of transportation.

I use one mostly for trips to the veterinarian or for any short run around town. For longer car trips (three hours or more), we usually take the cage instead.

Our friend Patrick (page 63) uses the carrier for all travels, long or short. He has traveled by plane, train, bus and car. Most of the time it was legal, but sometimes he was smuggled on board with a blanket tossed over his carrier. Beth says that different transportation lines have different rules, but she tries to take him as her carry-on luggage whenever she can. She is not opposed to checking him through cargo when she is certain that

**ON THE GO**
Patrick likes to explore new places and meet new people. He willingly hops into his carrier, ready for an excursion with Beth.

# "If you want your bunny loose in the car, it may require a few special training sessions..."

the cargo room has temperature control.

When Amy Millan was taking her mother's Christmas bunny from San Francisco to Los Angeles, she paid the extra twenty dollars for special handling of her "cargo." She didn't want her bunny's carrier put on the conveyer belt, and she felt that having it hand delivered to her after the flight was worth the money.

## CAR COMFORT

For automobile travel, a carrier is not an absolute necessity. Sandy (page 54) went clear across the country just sitting on the back seat of the car. If you want your bunny loose in the car, it may require a few special training sessions prior to starting out on a long trip. We tried this once, and our rabbit behaved the same way as our cat by crawling under the seat and not coming out until we had reached our destination.

A word of caution for traveling in very hot weather. The excitement of traveling seems to make rabbits hotter than ever, and without air-conditioning, it can be very uncomfortable and even dangerous. If you must take your rabbit on summer travels, you can use one of the cooling methods mentioned on page 100.

## TRAVEL SNACKS

Most rabbits don't like to eat while they're actually on the move, but some treat with a high moisture content (like a carrot or an apple) should be available if they want it. It may take a while after the motion has stopped to get back onto pellet bowl and water bottle.

When Dena and Bob Sharp made the trip from California to South Carolina, they were on the road for 48 hours straight. When they got to the first motel, their rabbit Sandy ate and drank and used her litter box and seemed very glad to be stopped at last. For the rest of the trip, through South Carolina and down into Georgia, moving from lodging to lodging, Sandy quickly made herself at home wherever they stopped. She took care of her feeding and toilet needs and braced herself for another day of travel. By the time they started back to California, Sandy was an experienced traveler and sat up on an ice chest in the back seat and looked out the window. This was a winter trip, so high temperatures were not a problem.

Sandy and her daughter, Muffin, now go on summer camping trips and keep themselves cool by taking a swim.

# Inward Mobility

YOU HAVE SEEN that your house rabbit can go up, down, and out into the world. He can go many places, but the most important is into your heart.

As he burrows in deeper and deeper, you will find that in providing for his well-being, you will be providing for your own. You will thank him for the bother he causes you. How can I explain this logically? I can't. As you mend the rug or repair a piece of woodwork, you too will be hard pressed to explain to others what your house rabbit is giving you. Yet, you know there's something there that makes you so look forward to coming home to it. You know you will feel that soothing ointment on all your little wounds of the day. That monumental pile of stresses you've been accumulating will, if not disappear, at least diminish in size.

Those of us whose rabbits occupy our hearts and homes know the power of these quiet creatures. They have brought us not only down to our knees but prostrate to the floor. Yes, you'll wind up there too. No one is exempt from this absurdity. Whatever your social standing or economic worth, you will be brought to the floor like everyone else who lives with a house rabbit. But from this lower

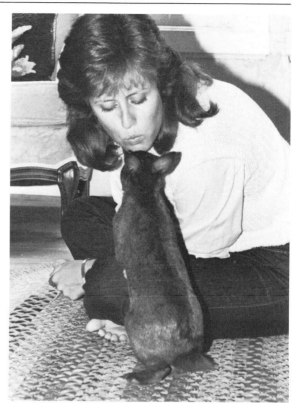

vantage point you may see things in the proper perspective. You will begin to restructure your priorities when your house rabbit points out to you that you have been placing value on the wrong things. After all, what can be more important than petting a rabbit?

# Index